Luke Prodromou with Audrey Cowan

FLASH
on English

ELEMENTARY
STUDENT'S BOOK

ELi

Welcome to Flash on English

Flash on English is your new English language course. On these two pages you will find some information to help you learn to use your text book.

The **Starter Unit** is the opening unit which will help you revise the English basics that you have studied previously.

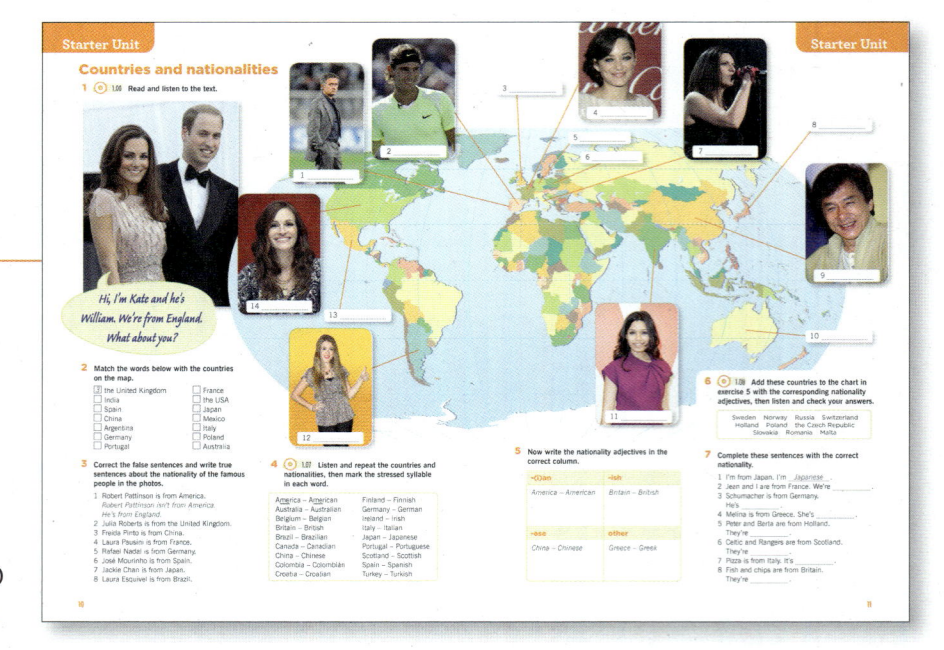

Flash on English contains 10 units, organised in this way:

Flash Forward activities keep fast finishers busy.

Double linguistic input
- Each unit opens with a **first presentation text** which can be in various formats (article, email, report).
- The **second presentation text** is in the form of a dialogue with a photostory. This follows the daily life of a group of London teenagers who are dealing with their day-to-day problems and aspirations for the future.
- Examples of grammatical structures and functions are presented in the **Grammar** and the **Functions** boxes, in a concise and clear form to allow the student full autonomy in carrying out the activities.
- The **Flashpoint** box highlights particular language structures that are commonly used.

WB p. 8 refers to the correspondent exercises in the **Workbook**

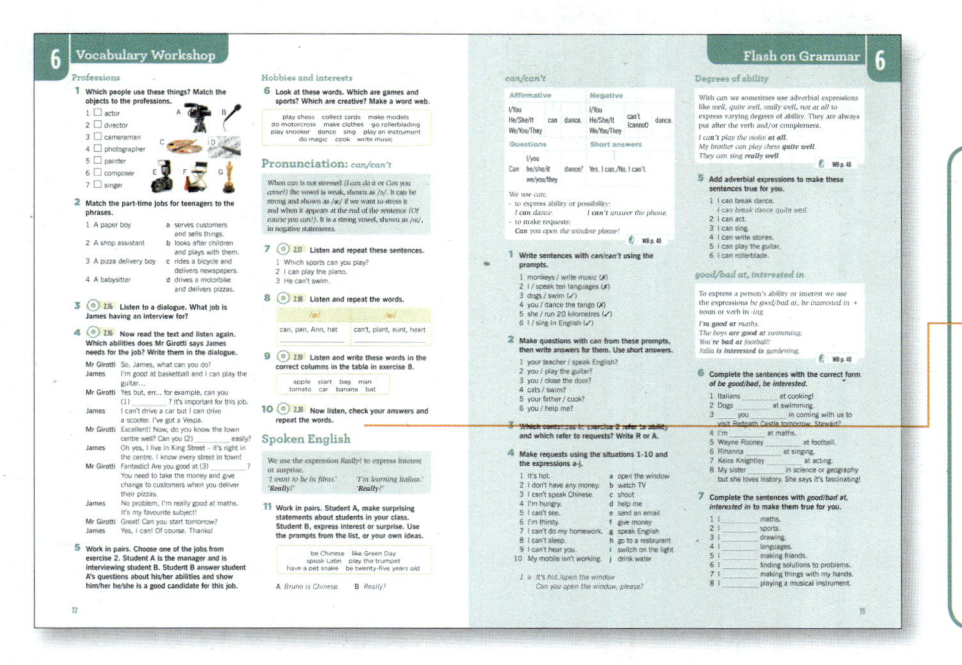

The **Vocabulary Workshop** page helps to expand and consolidate the lexis from each unit.

- The **Spoken English** section familiarises students with colloquial expressions used by native speakers.

The **Flash on Grammar** page is dedicated to presenting the grammar structures.

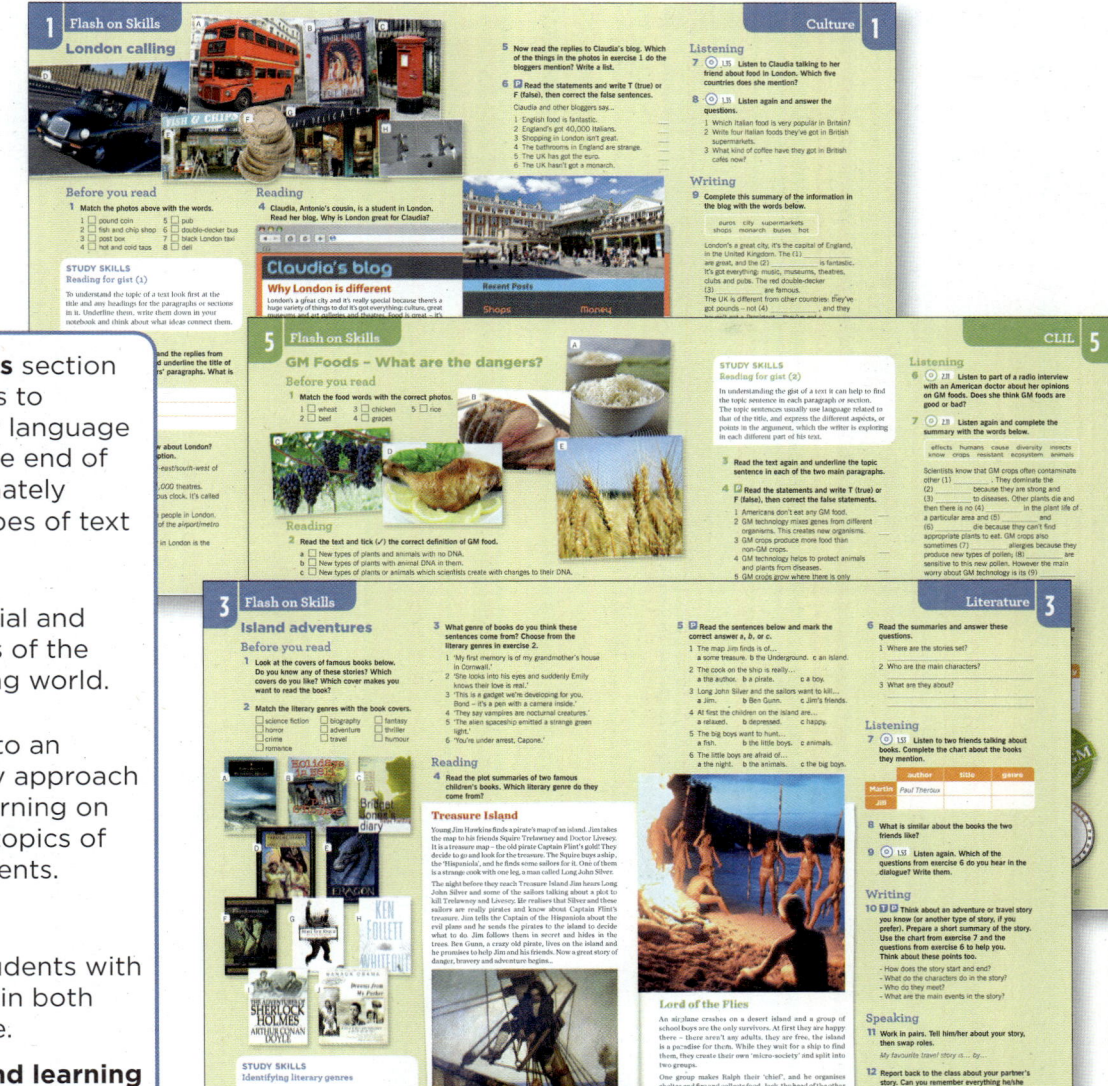

The **Flash on Skills** section helps the students to develop their four language skills. Placed at the end of each unit, it alternately presents three types of text material.

- **CULTURE**
  Focuses on social and cultural aspects of the English-speaking world.
- **CLIL**
  Texts targeted to an interdisciplinary approach to language learning on contemporary topics of interest to students.
- **LITERATURE**
  Texts aimed at familiarising students with literary genres, in both prose and verse.

Effective **study and learning techniques** are presented in each unit.

Contents

Starter Unit p. 8	**Grammar:** *be*, *have got*, plural nouns, possessive *'s*, possessive adjectives, *there is/are*, *this/these/that/tho* imperatives, *a/an/the*

Unit	Grammar	Vocabulary	Functions
1 Bright Lights, Big City p. 24	*be* *have got* Wh- questions + *be* Possessive adjectives Possessive *'s*	Personal possessions The family	Talking about personal possessions Giving personal information
2 Home Life p. 32	Present simple Prepositions of time Prepositions of place	Daily activities Rooms and furniture Verbs of daily routine	Talking about daily routines Describing a room
Flashback 1-2 p. 40			
3 My Ideal Holiday p. 42	Adverbs of frequency Verbs of preference + *-ing* Object pronouns	Holiday activities Holiday accommodation Transport	Expressing preferences Asking for travel information
4 What's in Fashion? p. 50	Present continuous Present continuous vs Present simple	Clothes and accessories Adjectives for clothes	Describing people's clothes Shopping for clothes
Flashback 3-4 p. 58			
5 You Are What You Eat... p. 60	Countable/uncountable nouns *some/any* *How much/many...?* *too much/many* *a lot of, a little, a few* *not much/many, enough*	Food and drink Containers and packages	Talking about food preferences Talking about quantities
6 They've Got Talent! p. 68	*can/can't* Degrees of ability *good/bad at, interested in*	Professions Hobbies and interests	Talking about abilities and interests
Flashback 5-6 p. 76			

Vocabulary: greetings and introductions, countries and nationalities, colours, the English alphabet, personal possessions, the family, classroom objects, classroom language, cardinal numbers, ordinal numbers, days of the week, months and seasons, the time

Pronunciation/ Spoken English	Skills	Study Skills
/h/	**Culture - London calling** **Reading** A personal blog **Listening** A conversation about food **Writing** A paragraph about a city **Speaking** Ask and answer questions about a city	Recording vocabulary Reading for gist (1)
/s/ /ɪz/ /z/ Exclamations: *Wow!*, *Cool!*, *Wicked!*, *Bummer!*	**CLIL - A land and its people** **Reading** An article about the Inuit **Listening** An interview with an Inuit boy **Writing** A summary **Speaking** Comparing cultures	Making a word web Identifying text types
/ŋ/	**Literature - Island adventures** **Reading** Plot summaries **Listening** A conversation about books **Writing** A summary of a book **Speaking** Favourite books	Writing word definitions Identifying literary genres
/tʃ/ and /ʃ/ Exclamations with *What* (*a/an*) + adjective	**Culture - Retail therapy** **Reading** An online article about shopping in Britain **Listening** A woman talking about an unusual shop **Writing** Information for tourists **Speaking** Report about shopping in your area	Using a dictionary (1) Taking notes
word stress	**CLIL - GM Foods - What are the dangers?** **Reading** A text about GM foods **Listening** A doctor talking about GM foods **Writing** A summary of a radio interview **Speaking** A discussion about GM foods	Reading for gist (2)
can/can't Use of *Really?*	**Literature - *The Commitments*** **Reading** An extract from the book **Listening** An interview with a band **Speaking** A class discussion about forming a band **Writing** A paragraph about a favourite band	Listening for specific information

Contents

Unit	Grammar	Vocabulary	Functions
7 Love, Love, Love... p. 78	Past simple: *be* *was/were born* *can* for permission *be like*	Life events Physical appearance Adjectives of personality	Talking about changes from past to present Describing appearance and personality
8 Out and About p. 86	Past simple: affirmative, negative and interrogative forms Past simple: regular and irregular verbs	Adjectives in *-ing* and *-ed* Emotions	Talking about past events Expressing feelings
Flashback 7-8 p. 94			
9 Is it Chance? p. 96	Past continuous Adverbs of manner	Professions Crimes and criminals	Talking about temporary events in the past
10 Money p. 104	Compounds of *some*, *any*, *no*, *every* Possessive pronouns *Whose...?* *like* and *would like*	Shopping At the restaurant	Asking for information Ordering in a restaurant
Flashback 9-10 p. 112			
Appendix p. 114			
Audioscripts p. 116			

Pronunciation/ Spoken English	Skills	Study Skills
Stress on word prefixes	**Culture - They're coming out of the kitchen...** **Reading** An article about famous British women **Listening** A description of a person's life **Speaking** A memory test **Writing** A biographical paragraph	Making opposite adjectives Writing a short biography
Past simple -ed Use of *a bit*	**CLIL - Victorian London** **Reading** A historical text **Listening** A radio programme **Speaking** Unusual jobs **Writing** A paragraph about life in the past	Using a dictionary (2) Planning your writing
/ə/ (1)	**Literature - *Frankenstein's Monster*** **Reading** Three episodes of a book **Listening** A student talking about *Frankenstein* **Speaking** Book themes **Writing** Describing a scene of a book	Writing example sentences Opening sentences
/ə/ (2) Apologising	**Culture - Pocket money** **Reading** An online article about pocket money **Listening** A radio presenter talking about British teens **Speaking** A conversation about spending habits **Writing** A survey about spending habits	Annotating visual information

Starter Unit

Greetings and introductions

1 Read and complete with the words below.

| years | I'm | from | Hi |

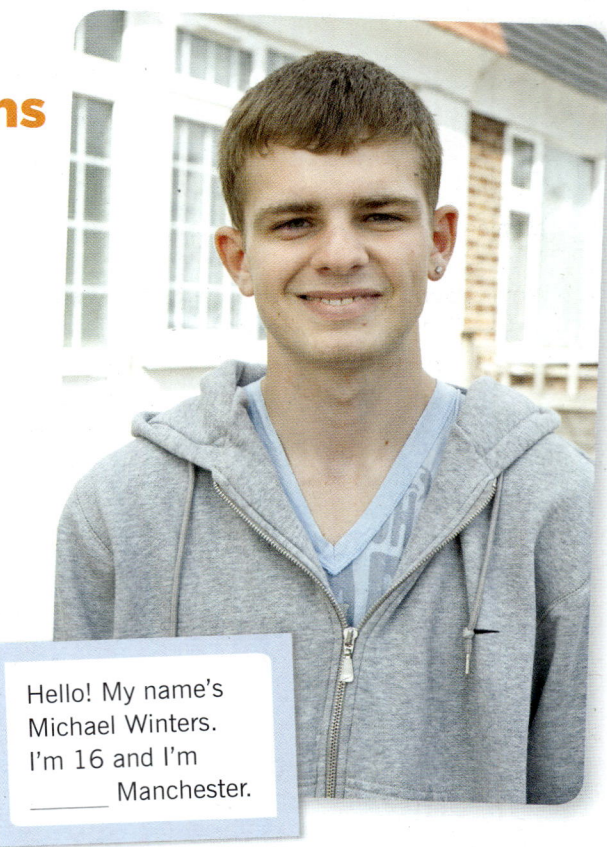

Hi, _____ Antonio Clark. I'm 16 years old and I'm from Liverpool.

Hello! My name's Michael Winters. I'm 16 and I'm _____ Manchester.

_____, I'm Anna, Anna Harrison. I'm 16. I'm from London.

Hello, my name's Robyn MacGregor. I'm 16 _____ old and I'm from Edinburgh.

2 🔊 1.02 Listen and check.

3 True or false? Write T or F.
1 Antonio is 15 years old. ____
2 Michael is from Liverpool. ____
3 Anna is Italian. ____
4 Robyn is 16 years old. ____

8

Starter Unit

Introducing yourself and others

4 🔊 1.03 **Listen and repeat.**

Paolo   Hello, I'm Paolo.
Monica   Hi, my name's Monica.

5 Now practise introductions with other students in the class. Use your own names.

6 🔊 1.04 **Listen and repeat.**

Luca   Paolo, this is Monica.
Monica   Hi, Paolo. Nice to meet you.
Paolo   Hello, Monica.

7 Practise the dialogues in groups of three. Use your names. Take it in turns.

Greeting people

Hello./Hi./Hey.	Nice to meet you.	My name's…
Good morning.	Pleased to meet you.	I'm…
Good afternoon.	Good to see you.	
Good evening.		
How are you?	I'm fine, thank you.	
How's it going?	Fine, thanks.	
	I'm OK, thanks.	
	Very well.	
	Alright.	
	Not too bad.	

Saying goodbye

| Bye./Bye-bye. | See you. |
| Goodbye. | Good night. |

8 Look at the tables and underline the formal expressions.

9 🔊 1.05 **Listen and repeat.**

A Hi, how are you?
B I'm fine thanks. And you?
A I'm OK.

10 Now practise the dialogue in ex. 9 with a partner. Change the words in blue to make new dialogues. Use the information in the tables to help you.

11 Look at the situations in the photos and make dialogues.

A

B

be: affirmative and negative

12 Complete the chart.

Affirmative		
I	am/'m	
He/She/It	is/____	from Italy.
You/We/They	____/'re	
Negative		
I	____/'m not	
He/She/It	____/isn't	from England.
You/We/They	are not/____	

13 Complete the sentences with the correct form of the verb *to be*.

1 I '*m* from France.
2 I _____ a doctor.
3 You _____ 21 years old.
4 She _____ from France.
5 We _____ in England.
6 They _____ actors.
7 She _____ Elizabeth Jones.
8 Silvia and I _____ friends.
9 Cate and Kristen _____ doctors.

14 Change the sentences above from affirmative to negative.

1 *I'm not from France.*

Starter Unit

Countries and nationalities

1 🔊 **1.06** Read and listen to the text.

Hi, I'm Kate and he's William. We're from England. What about you?

2 Match the words below with the countries on the map.

- [3] the United Kingdom
- [ ] India
- [ ] Spain
- [ ] China
- [ ] Argentina
- [ ] Germany
- [ ] Portugal
- [ ] France
- [ ] the USA
- [ ] Japan
- [ ] Mexico
- [ ] Italy
- [ ] Poland
- [ ] Australia

3 Correct the false sentences and write true sentences about the nationality of the famous people in the photos.

1 Robert Pattinson is from America.
   Robert Pattinson isn't from America. He's from England.
2 Julia Roberts is from the United Kingdom.
3 Freida Pinto is from China.
4 Laura Pausini is from France.
5 Rafael Nadal is from Germany.
6 José Mourinho is from Spain.
7 Jackie Chan is from Japan.
8 Laura Esquivel is from Brazil.

4 🔊 **1.07** Listen and repeat the countries and nationalities, then mark the stressed syllable in each word.

America – American	Finland – Finnish
Australia – Australian	Germany – German
Belgium – Belgian	Ireland – Irish
Britain – British	Italy – Italian
Brazil – Brazilian	Japan – Japanese
Canada – Canadian	Portugal – Portuguese
China – Chinese	Scotland – Scottish
Colombia – Colombian	Spain – Spanish
Croatia – Croatian	Turkey – Turkish

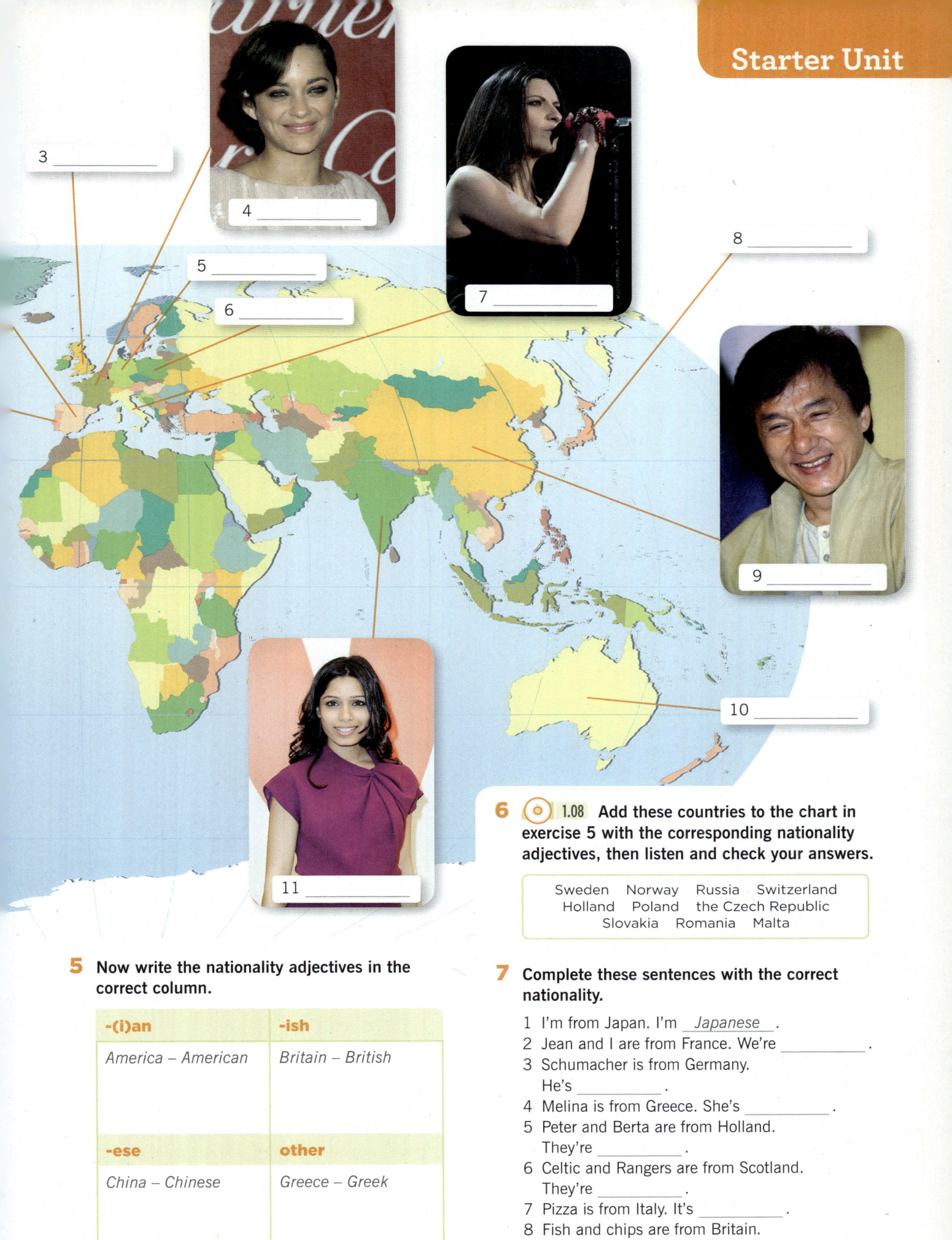

Starter Unit

3 _____
4 _____
5 _____
6 _____
7 _____
8 _____
9 _____
10 _____
11 _____

5 Now write the nationality adjectives in the correct column.

-(i)an	-ish
America – American	Britain – British

-ese	other
China – Chinese	Greece – Greek

6 🔊 1.08 Add these countries to the chart in exercise 5 with the corresponding nationality adjectives, then listen and check your answers.

> Sweden   Norway   Russia   Switzerland
> Holland   Poland   the Czech Republic
> Slovakia   Romania   Malta

7 Complete these sentences with the correct nationality.

1 I'm from Japan. I'm _Japanese_.
2 Jean and I are from France. We're _____.
3 Schumacher is from Germany. He's _____.
4 Melina is from Greece. She's _____.
5 Peter and Berta are from Holland. They're _____.
6 Celtic and Rangers are from Scotland. They're _____.
7 Pizza is from Italy. It's _____.
8 Fish and chips are from Britain. They're _____.

Starter Unit

be: questions and short answers

1 Complete the table.

Questions		
_____	I	from the USA?
Is	he/she/it	
Are	you/we/they	
Short answers		
Yes, I am./No, I'm not.		
Yes, he/she/it _____./No, he/she/it isn't.		
Yes, you/we/they _____./No, you/we/they _____.		

2 Make three questions and answers from these prompts.

1 France / Italy / Rome
   Are you from France? No, I'm not.
   Are you from Italy? Yes, I am.
   Where are you from in Italy? I'm from Rome.
2 Spain / France / Marseilles
3 Switzerland / Germany / Berlin
4 Mexico / Argentina / Buenos Aires
5 England / Scotland / Glasgow
6 Greece / Russia / Moscow
7 Holland / Belgium / Brussels

3 🔊 **1.09** Listen to the phone conversation and fill in the gaps with a word or phrase.

A Hi, where are you now? Are (1) _____ out?
B No, I'm not. I'm in my bedroom. (2) _____ are you?
A (3) _____ on the bus.
B Where's Laura?
A (4) _____ at home.
B Where (5) _____ your mum and dad?
A They're at work.
B (6) _____ Paolo with you?
A No, he's not.

4 Now practise the dialogue in exercise 3 with a partner. Change the words in blue to make new dialogues. Use these prompts.

> in the kitchen   in the living room
> in the park   in town   at school
> on the train   at the cafeteria
> at the cinema

> Katie   Julia   Brian and Catrin
> Simon and Mark

5 Complete the blanks with the nationality of these motorcycle drivers.

GRAND PRIX MOTORCYCLE RACING			
Position	Name		Nationality
1	Casey Stoner		
2	Jorge Lorenzo		
3	Andrea Dovizioso		
4	Dani Pedrosa		
5	Ben Spies		

6 Look at the results board and ask and answer.

A *Who's he?*
B *Casey Stoner.*
A *Where's he from?*
B *He's Australian./He's from Australia.*

7 🔊 **1.10** Listen and complete the dialogue.

A What (1) _____ your name?
B Javier Bardem.
A Are you from Argentina?
B No, I'm (2) _____.
A Where are you from?
B I'm from (3) _____.
A Ah, you're Spanish.
B Yes, I am. And you? (4) _____ your name?
A I'm Julia Roberts.
B Are you from Canada?
A No, (5) _____ not.
B Where are you from?
A I'm from the USA.
B Ah, you're (6) _____.

8 Now in pairs, practise the dialogue.

9 Imagine you're a famous celebrity from another country. Choose a name, a country and a nationality and complete the form.

Your name	
Country	
Nationality	

10 Can your partner guess which celebrity you are? Ask and answer. Use the dialogue in exercise 7 to help you.

Starter Unit

Colours

1 Write the names of the colours.

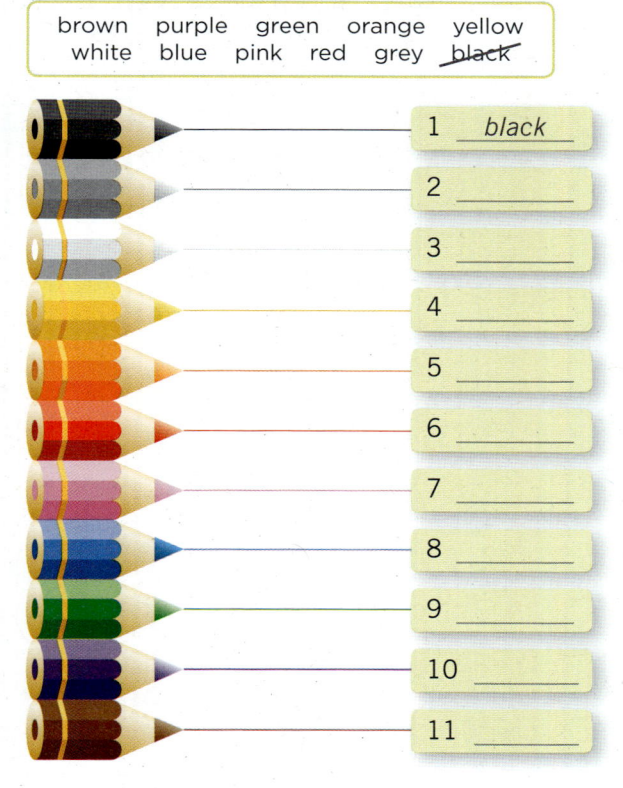

> brown   purple   green   orange   yellow
> white   blue   pink   red   grey   black

1. black
2. ___
3. ___
4. ___
5. ___
6. ___
7. ___
8. ___
9. ___
10. ___
11. ___

2 🔊 1.11 Which flag is it? Listen and write the number.

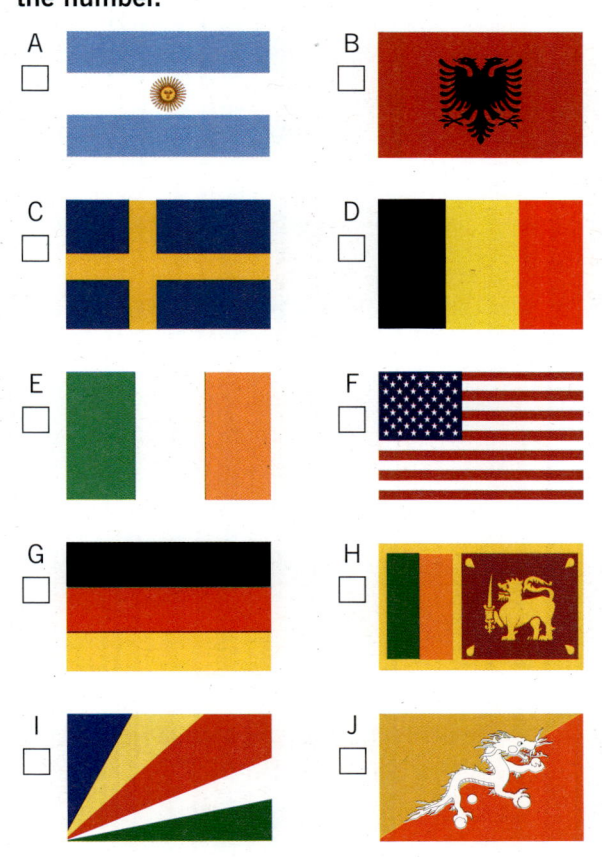

A ☐   B ☐
C ☐   D ☐
E ☐   F ☐
G ☐   H ☐
I ☐   J ☐

3 Now describe a flag. Can your partner guess it?

The English alphabet

4 Complete the missing letters.

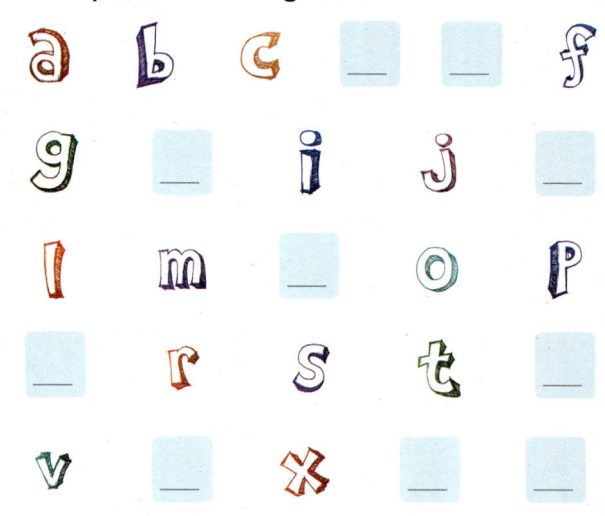

a   b   c   ___   ___   f
g   ___   i   j   ___
l   m   ___   o   p
___   r   s   t   ___
v   ___   x   ___

5 🔊 1.12 Now listen and check. Repeat the letters.

6 Which letters rhyme, or have got the same sound? Write them in the correct groups. Which letters don't go in any of the groups?

A	H _ _
B	C _ _ _ _ _ _
F	L _ _ _ _
I	_
Q	_ _

7 Work in pairs, ask and answer.

A *What's your surname?*
B *Rogers.*
A *How do you spell it?*
B *R-O-G-E-R-S.*

Game!

8 Think of a word for a country. Write it on a piece of paper. Your partner guesses the word, letter by letter. The person who guesses using fewer letters wins.

A *E?*
B *Yes.*
A *I?*
B *No!!*

13

Starter Unit

Personal possessions

have got – all forms

1 🔊 **1.13** Listen and read the dialogue, then complete the chart.

Official	Have you got a laptop?
Passenger	No, I haven't. But I've got an MP3.
Official	Have you got liquids, water or shampoo in your bag?
Passenger	Yes, I have…

Affirmative			**Negative**		
I/You/We/They He/She/It	have got/_____ has got/'s got	an MP3.	I/You/We/They He/She/It	have not got/ haven't got _____ / hasn't got	an MP3.

Questions				**Short answers**
_____ Has	I/you/we/they he/she/it	got	an MP3?	Yes, I have./No, I _____ . Yes, he has./No, he hasn't.

2 Match the words with the pictures.
- ☐ mobile ☐ camera ☐ MP3 player
- ☐ comb ☐ sunglasses ☐ iPod
- ☐ watch ☐ laptop ☐ wallet

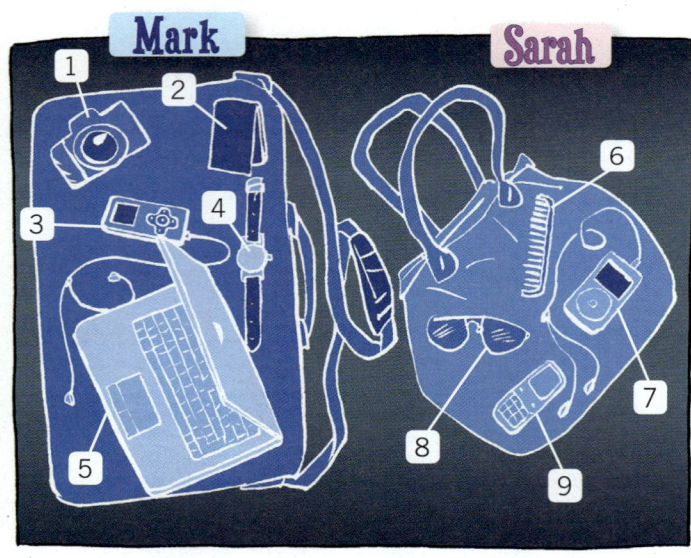

Mark 1 2 3 4 5 **Sarah** 6 7 8 9

3 🔊 **1.14** Listen and check your answers.

4 Who am I, Mark or Sarah?
1 I've got a mobile and a comb.   Sarah
2 I've got an MP3. I haven't got an iPod. _____
3 I haven't got a comb. I've got a watch. _____
4 I haven't got a camera. I've got sunglasses. _____
5 I haven't got a mobile phone. I've got a laptop. _____
6 I've got a wallet. I haven't got a comb. _____

5 Look at the pictures in ex. 2 and, in pairs, take turns to ask and answer questions with *have got*.

A *Has Sarah got a mobile?*
B *Yes, she has.*
B *Has Mark got an iPod?*
A *No, he hasn't.*

6 Fill in the information about you, then ask and answer with a partner.

		you	partner
Have you got	a mobile?		
	a CD player?		
	a bike?		
	a radio?		
	a watch?		
	a camera?		
	a laptop?		

A *Have you got a mobile?*
B *Yes, I have./No, I haven't.*

7 Write sentences about you and your partner with *have got/haven't got*.

1 *I've got a mobile.*
  Laura hasn't got a mobile.

14

Starter Unit

Plural nouns

8 Complete the chart.

Singular	Plural
baby	babies
child	_____
tooth	teeth
foot	_____
shoe	_____
man	_____
woman	women
box	boxes
person	_____
mouse	_____
watch	_____

9 🔊 1.15 Listen and check your answers.

10 Complete the sentences with words from exercise 8.
1. Tim Robbins has got two _____, John and Miles.
2. Human beings have got two hands and two _____.
3. Two _____ have got four hands and four feet.
4. New _____ haven't got teeth.
5. We've got 28-32 _____.
6. The managers in that company are all _____, there isn't one woman!
7. She hasn't got _____ on her feet, she's got sandals.
8. Our French and English teachers are _____, Miss Joanna Smith and Miss Anna Jones.
9. There are 20 _____ of chocolates in this cupboard.
10. Mickey, Jerry and Stuart Little are famous _____.

Possessive 's

We use the possessive 's to express possession or family relations.

- After a singular noun we add 's.
  That's Jimi Hendrix's guitar.
- After a plural noun we normally add 's.
  These are my children's cousins.
- After a plural noun ending in -s, we add only the apostrophe.
  My grandparents' house is in Rome.

11 Look at the pictures and complete the sentences with the possessive form of the names below.

> Batman   Prince William   Valentino Rossi
> Elvis   James Bond   Bono Vox

1. ☐ She's _____ wife.
2. ☐ It's _____ car.
3. ☐ It's _____ mask.
4. ☐ It's _____ motorbike.
5. ☐ They're _____ glasses.
6. ☐ It's _____ gold suit.

15

Starter Unit

The family

1 🔊 **1.16** Listen and read the texts, then complete the family trees.

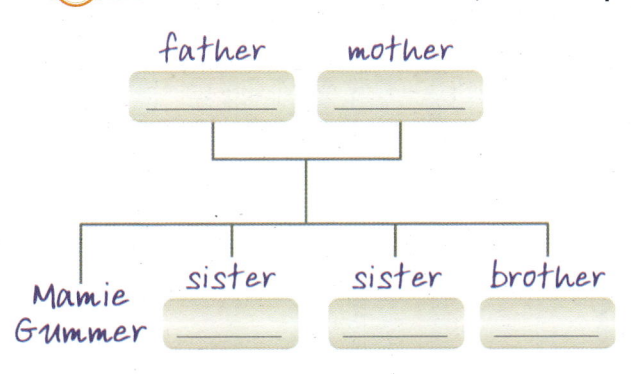

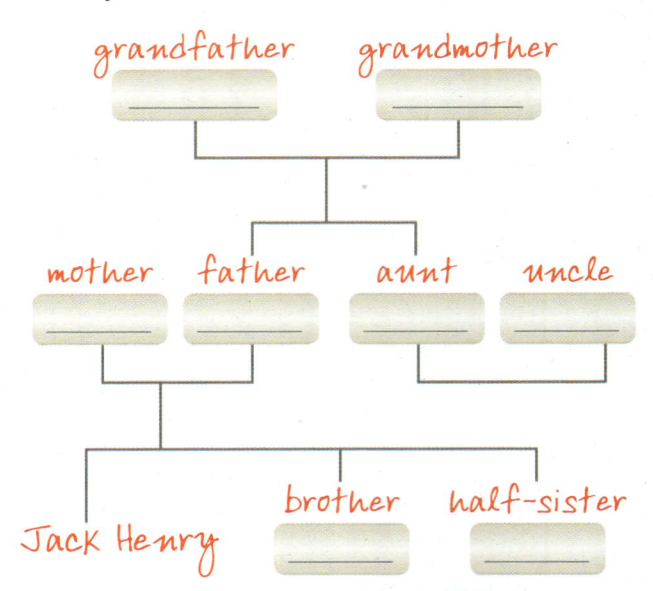

```
    father    mother                    grandfather   grandmother
      |_____|                            |_____|
           |                                        |
   _____              _____
   |        |        |             |         |         |          |
 Mamie    sister   sister  brother mother  father     aunt      uncle
 Gummer                            
                                          |_____|
                                               |
                                        _____
                                        |        |        |
                                     Jack     brother  half-sister
                                     Henry
```

Mamie Gummer

Mamie Gummer is an actress. Her mother is Meryl Streep, the famous actress. Her father is Don Gummer. She has got two sisters, Louise and Grace Gummer; Grace is also an actress. Her brother is Henry, a singer and songwriter.

Jack Henry Robbins

Jack Henry Robbins is an actor. He is from a family of actors and musicians. He is the son of two famous stars. His father's name is Tim Robbins, the actor and his mother is Susan Sarandon, the actress. Jack Henry's grandfather, Gil, is a musician. His grandmother, Mary, is an actress. Jack Henry has got a brother, Miles Robbins. He's a singer in a rock band. He's got a half-sister, Eva Amurri. Eva is an actress and she's the daughter of an Italian director, Franco Amurri, and Susan Sarandon. His aunt, Tim Robbins' sister, Adele, is an actress. His uncle, David Robbins, Tim Robbins' brother, is a musician.

Starter Unit

2 Read the information in exercise 1 again and complete the sentences with the words below.

♂	♀
father	mother
son	daughter
brother	sister
uncle	aunt
husband	wife
grandfather	grandmother
grandson	granddaughter
nephew	niece

1 Miles is Jack Henry's _____ .
2 Don Gummer is Meryl Streep's _____ .
3 Susan Sarandon is Eva Amurri's _____ .
4 Adele is Tim Robbin's _____ .
5 Adele is Jack Henry's _____ .
6 Jack Henry is Adele's _____ .
7 Meryl is Don's _____ .
8 Jack Henry is Gil's _____ .
9 Mary is Jack Henry's _____ .
10 Gil is Miles' _____ .

3 🔘 1.17 Listen and check your answers.

Game!

4 Who am I? Choose a person from exercise 1. Don't tell your partner. Answer your partner's questions. Can he/she guess who you are?

A *Have you got children?*
B *Yes, I have.*
A *Have you got two children?*
B *No, I haven't.*
A *Have you got a son called Jack Henry?*
B *Yes, I have.*
A *You're Tim Robbins.*
B *Yes, I am.*

Possessive adjectives

5 Complete the chart.

Subject pronouns	Possessive adjectives
I	my
you	_____
he	his
she	_____
_____	its
we	_____
_____	their

6 Rewrite the sentences with the correct possessive adjective.

1 I've got dark hair. _My_ hair is dark.
2 Tom's got brown shoes. _____ shoes are brown.
3 You've got a new mobile phone! _____ mobile is new!
4 You've got black bags. _____ bags are black.
5 We've got a nice teacher. _____ teacher is nice.
6 They've got a house in London. _____ house is in London.
7 Jamie has got a pet mouse. _____ pet is a mouse.
8 I've got two cousins in Canada. _____ cousins are in Canada.

7 Complete the email with personal pronouns and possessive adjectives.

Hi, Rosa!
Thanks for the message. (1) _I_ 'm from Germany and (2) _____ full name is Ralf Fischer. I've got a brother and a sister. (3) _____ brother is Markus and (4) _____ 's 13 years old. (5) _____ sister is Brigit and (6) _____ 's 16 years old. We've got a dog. (7) _____ name is Whitie because (8) _____ 's white! (9) _____ mum and dad are teachers. (10) _____ are called Frank and Claudia. My best friends are Maria and Peter. (11) _____ are brother and sister. (12) _____ house is next door to our house. (13) _____ parents are good friends, too.

17

Starter Unit

My school life

1 Complete the dialogue with the words below.

> class   is   name   nice   hi

A Rod, this is Laura.
B (1) _____ , Laura. I'm Rod.
C Nice to meet you.
B (2) _____ to meet you, too. What class are you in?
C I'm in (3) _____ 10A.
B Yeah? My cousin (4) _____ in that class!
C What's his name?
B She's a girl. Her (5) _____ 's Julie Macintosh.
C Julie Macintosh? She's nice.

2 🔊 1.18   Now listen and check.

3 Practise the dialogue from exercise 1 in groups of three. Change the words in blue to make new dialogues.

Classroom objects

4 Match the things in the picture with the words below.

> whiteboard   desk   textbook   eraser   pencil   sharpener
> locker   pencil case   bin   board pen   folder   notebook

5 🔊 1.19   Now listen, check your answers and repeat the words.

Starter Unit

there is/are

6 Complete the chart.

Affirmative	Negative
There is a man at the door.	There isn't a cinema in my town.
There are two girls in my science class.	There _____ two books in my bag.

Questions	Short answer
_____ there an apple in the cupboard?	Yes, there is./ No, there _____.
Are there five dogs or four?	Yes, there _____./ No, there aren't.

7 What things are there in your classroom? Write true sentences. Use *there is/are*.

1 whiteboard
2 desk
3 computer
4 eraser
5 bag
6 pencil
7 sharpener
8 locker
9 bin
10 board pen
11 folder
12 chair

1 *There isn't a whiteboard, there's a blackboard.*

this/these, that/those

We use **this/these** to refer to objects or people that are close to the speaker; we use **that/those** to refer to objects or people that are a distance away from the speaker.

8 Read the dialogues.

Teacher What's this?
Pupil   This is a whiteboard.

Teacher What's that?
Pupil   That's a desk.

Teacher What are these?
Pupil   These are textbooks.

Teacher What are those?
Pupil   Those are bins.

9 Ask and answer with a partner about things in your classroom.

A *What's this?*
B *It's a whiteboard.*
A *What's that?*
B *It's a desk.*

10 Choose the correct answer, *this*, *that*, *these* or *those*.

1 *This/Those* is a red pen, not a blue pen.
2 *That/This* is Richard's desk in the centre of the classroom.
3 *That/Those* are our new textbooks on the desk there.
4 Is *this/these* your sharpener, Louise?
5 The computer is in *that/these* cupboard.
6 My homework exercise is in *this/those* notebook, not the yellow notebook.

11 Work with a partner. Student A, look at the things in picture A. Which words do you not know in English? Make questions with *this*, *that*, *these*, *those* to ask your partner. Student B, look at the objects in picture B and make similar questions.

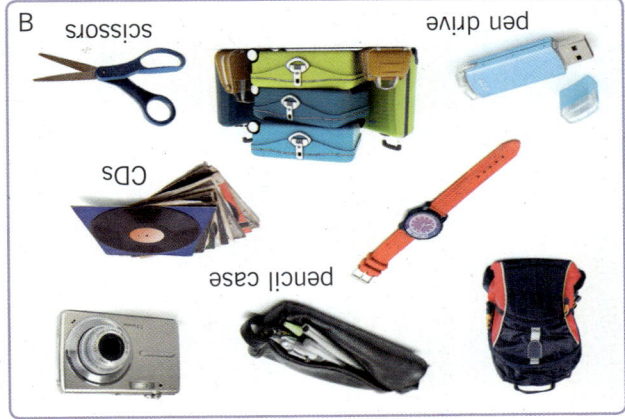

A
backpack
camera
watch
suitcases

B
scissors
pen drive
CDs
pencil case

A *Excuse me, what's this?*
B *That's a pencil case.*

B *Excuse me, what's that?*
A *This is a backpack.*

19

Starter Unit

Imperatives

Affirmative	Negative
Go!	Don't go!

We use the imperative to give orders or instructions.

Open the door!
Don't write on your textbook!
Close your books and listen to the recording.

Classroom language

1 Complete the sentences with the words from the list.

> sit   open   write   close (x2)   look   put   work

1 _Open_ the door.
2 _____ in your notebook.
3 _____ in pairs.
4 _____ your book.
5 _____ down.
6 _____ at the board.
7 _____ your hands up.
8 _____ your eyes.

2 Make the commands in exercise 1 negative.

1 *Don't open the door.*

3 🔘 1.20 Listen and repeat.

1 Stand up.
2 Sit down.
3 Put your hands up.
4 Open your books!
5 Close your books.
6 Open your bags.
7 Close your bags.
8 Put your left hand up.
9 Switch the light on.
10 Touch your hair.
11 Take your coat off.
12 Stop the CD player.

Game!

4 Student A choose examples from exercise 3 and give your partner commands. Student B, listen and mime the command.

5 Read the following expressions and translate them into your own language.

1 Open the window, please.   _T_
2 Close the door.   ___
3 Write the answers in your notebook. ___
4 Please, be quiet.   ___
5 Don't shout.   ___
6 How do we say that in English? ___
7 I don't understand.   ___
8 Where's your homework?   ___
9 May I leave the room?   ___
10 How do we spell…?   ___
11 Clean the board, please.   ___
12 Can you repeat that, please?   ___

1 _____
2 _____
3 _____
4 _____
5 _____
6 _____
7 _____
8 _____
9 _____
10 _____
11 _____
12 _____

6 Read the English sentences in exercise 5 again. Underline the imperative forms. Who normally says these things, the teacher or the students? Write T, S or B (both).

Starter Unit

a/an/the

7 Find the words in the text. Underline the articles *a, an, the* in the text and the nouns they refer to.

> Hi, I'm from Durham. Durham is <u>a city</u> in England. Durham is near Scotland. It is a beautiful city. It's got a cathedral. A cathedral is a big church. The cathedral in Durham is very old. I'm a student in a secondary school in the city centre. The school is big. It is new.
>
> Our house is in a street near the centre. The street is 'Baker Street'. The house is 100 years old. My mum is a doctor. My dad's an engineer.
>
> I love food and my favourite food is Chinese. I go to a Chinese restaurant in Durham with my friends. The restaurant is called 'The Palace'.

- We use the indefinite article *a/an* when referring to a person's profession or occupation.
  *She's **a** doctor*
  *He's **an** engineer.*
  *I'm **a** pupil.*
- We use the definite article *the* when referring to specific objects or persons and the indefinite article *a/an* when speaking in general.
  *Give me **the** pen* (that pen on the table, for example).
  *Give me **a** pen* (it doesn't matter which pen).
- We use *a/an* when a person or a thing is mentioned for the first time, then when it is referred to again, we use *the*.
  *There's **a** dog in the park. **The** dog is black and very large.*

8 Write *a* or *an* in front of these nouns.

1. ____ teacher
2. ____ pupil
3. ____ aunt
4. ____ uncle
5. ____ architect
6. ____ actress
7. ____ toothbrush
8. ____ house
9. ____ MP3
10. ____ mobile phone
11. ____ apple
12. ____ folder

9 Complete the short text.

In (1) *the* park there is (2) *a* man. (3) ____ man is old. He has got (4) ____ dog. (5) ____ dog is big and black. There is (6) ____ woman. (7) ____ woman is young. She's got (8) ____ dog, too. (9) ____ dog is small and white. In (10) ____ park there is (11) ____ girl. (12) ____ girl has got (13) ____ tennis racket and an MP3. She hasn't got (14) ____ ball. The weather in (15) ____ park is nice. It's sunny.

10 Now write a description about you and your city.

> Hi, I'm from _____ . _____ is a city/town in _____ . _____ is near _____ . It is a _____ city. It's got _____ .
>
> I am a pupil in _____ school. The school is _____ . It is _____ .
>
> Our house is in _____ . My mum is _____ . My dad's _____ .
>
> I love _____ . My favourite _____ is _____ .

Starter Unit

NUMBERS

Cardinal numbers

1 Write the numbers in words.

1 _one_
2 _____
3 _____
4 _____
5 _____
6 _____
7 _____
8 _____
9 _____
10 _____

2 🔊 1.21 Mark the stressed syllables on these numbers, then listen and check.

11 eleven	50 fifty
12 twelve	60 sixty
13 thirteen	70 seventy
14 fourteen	80 eighty
15 fifteen	90 ninety
16 sixteen	100 a hundred
17 seventeen	101 a hundred and one
18 eighteen	102 a hundred and two
19 nineteen	200 two hundred
20 twenty	300 three hundred
30 thirty	900 nine hundred
40 forty	1000 a thousand

3 🔊 1.21 Listen again and repeat the numbers.

4 Write these numbers in figures.

a thirty-three _____
b eighty-eight _____
c twenty-two _____
d seventy-six _____
e twenty-six _____
f forty-three _____
g ninety-nine _____
h sixty-one _____
i fifty-two _____
j forty-six _____

5 🔊 1.22 Which numbers do you hear? Listen and underline the number.

1 a ten b two
2 a thirty b thirteen
3 a forty b fourteen
4 a fifty b fifteen
5 a sixty b sixteen
6 a seventeen b seventy
7 a eighteen b eighty
8 a nineteen b ninety
9 a nine hundred b a hundred

6 Write the answers in numbers and words.

1 Days in a week: _7, seven_.
2 Weeks in a month: _____.
3 Months in a year: _____.
4 Days in a month: _____.
5 Letters in the English alphabet: _____.
6 Pupils in your class: _____.
7 Pictures on the wall: _____.
8 Desks in the classroom: _____.
9 Windows in the classroom: _____.
10 Doors in the classroom: _____.

My fact file

7 🔊 1.23 Listen to the dialogue and complete Andy's answers.

Sam What's your mobile number?
Andy It's 6974201720.
Sam And your landline?
Andy (1) 1 ___ 03 66447 ___ .
Sam What's your home address?
Andy (2) _____ , George Street, Norwich NR ___ 1LT, UK.
Sam Are you on Facebook?
Andy Yeah, I've got (3) _____ Facebook friends.
Sam Wow! And what's your email?
Andy andy.maxwell@quickwebnet.uk
Sam Thanks. What's your favourite colour, Andy?
Andy Red.
Sam Okay, and your favourite number?
Andy 7.

8 Complete the information about you.

Mobile number: _____
Landline: _____
Home address: _____
email: _____
Favourite colour: _____
Favourite number: _____

9 Practise the dialogue in exercise 7 with a partner. Use the information you wrote in exercise 8.

A _What's your mobile number?_
B _It's 348 2891639._
A _And your landline?_
B _It's…_

Starter Unit

Ordinal numbers

10 🔘 **1.24** Listen and circle the numbers you hear.

21st 22nd 32nd 33rd 43rd 13th 30th

11 Write the figures next to the words.

eighth	___	fourth	___	sixth	___
eleven	___	ninth	___	tenth	___
fifth	___	second	___	third	___
first	*1st*	seventh	___	twelfth	___

Days of the week

12 Complete the sentences with the correct ordinal number.

1 The _____ day of the week is **Sunday**.
2 The _____ day of the week is **Saturday**.
3 The _____ day of the week is **Tuesday**.
4 The _____ day of the week is **Friday**.
5 The _____ day of the week is **Thursday**.
6 The _____ day of the week is **Wednesday**.
7 The _____ day of the week is **Monday**.

13 🔘 **1.25** Listen and check your answers.

Months and seasons

14 Complete the chart.

	Month	Short Form	Days	Season
1	January	Jan.	31	winter
2	_____	Feb.	28/29	_____
3	March	Mar.	_____	spring
4	April	Apr.	30	_____
5	May	May	_____	_____
6	June	Jun.	30	summer
7	_____	Jul.	31	_____
8	August	Aug.	31	_____
9	September	Sep.	30	_____
10	October	Oct.	31	autumn
11	_____	Nov.	30	autumn
12	December	Dec.	31	_____

15 In pairs, ask and answer.

A *When's your birthday?*
B *It's on the fourth of July.*

The time

16 🔘 **1.26** Listen and write the number next to the clock.

To tell time we always use the verb in the singular form with *it's*…
In the conventional version, we first say the minutes and then the hour:
It's five (minutes) past three.
It's a quarter to six.

In the digital version, we first say the hour and then the minutes: *It's five forty-five.*

In English we normally count the hours 1-12. To distinguish between morning and afternoon/ evening hours, we use the abbreviation *a.m.* (ante meridiem) or *p.m.* (post meridiem).
It's 5 a.m. in Los Angeles now, so it's 1 p.m. in London.

17 Match the times to the clocks.

A 09:00 B 09:50 C 02:45 D 02:30
E 01:25 F 05:55 G 07:15 H 11:48

1 ☐ It's half past two.
2 ☐ It's nine o'clock.
3 ☐ It's twelve minutes to twelve.
4 ☐ It's a quarter to three.
5 ☐ It's twenty-five past one.
6 ☐ It's ten to ten.
7 ☐ It's a quarter past seven.
8 ☐ It's five minutes to six.

18 Work in pairs. Ask and answer these times, then write them in words.

a 12.15   *a quarter past twelve*
b 6.35   _____
c 11.10   _____
d 8.20   _____
e 9.05   _____
f 3.45   _____

A *What time is it, please?*
B *It's a quarter past twelve.*

1 Bright Lights, Big City

Welcome to the LAC!

Vocabulary: Personal possessions

1 🔊 1.27 Listen and repeat the words. Which of these things are there in the picture? (✓)

- ☐ comb
- ☐ notebook
- ☐ ticket
- ☐ map
- ☐ digital camera
- ☐ diary
- ☐ laptop
- ☐ keys
- ☐ pen
- ☐ wallet
- ☐ MP3 player
- ☐ mobile phone
- ☐ cash card
- ☐ pencils
- ☐ passport

2 Which of the things in exercise 1 are for personal use and which are for use in class? Write them in the correct groups.

Personal use	Classroom use
_____	_____
_____	_____
_____	_____

3 🔊 1.28 Listen and read the text. What is the LAC?

4 Read the statements and write T (true) or F (false).

1. The LAC is a film studio. ____
2. The LAC hasn't got students from Britain. ____
3. Tony Harrison is the director of the LAC. ____
4. Hannah Hill is from Scotland. ____
5. The LAC has got a cinema. ____

FLASH FORWARD

Correct the false statements in exercise 4.

LONDON ARTS CENTRE

ABOUT LAC   COURSES   ADMISSIONS

What is the LAC?

The London Arts Centre is a famous film school for young people in central London. We have got excellent courses for actors, directors, designers, writers and technicians and we've got state-of-the-art technology and professional, experienced teachers.

- digital cameras for students
- video cameras for students
- laptop computers for all students
- access to film, animation and recording studios
- film library with 5,000 films

Who are our students?

The LAC isn't only a British school, it's an international school with students from all over the world. We've got students from Europe, Asia, Africa and America and of course from Britain! The classes are small and informal and all students for us are special.

Who are the directors of the school?

Hannah Hill, our new Academy Director, is a famous American producer and scriptwriter with years of experience at the Kerner Brothers studios in Hollywood. Hannah is also the teacher on the film writing course this year.

Tony Harrison our Assistant Director has got 20 years of experience in the theatres of London's West End as an actor and director. Tony is the drama and voice teacher at the school.

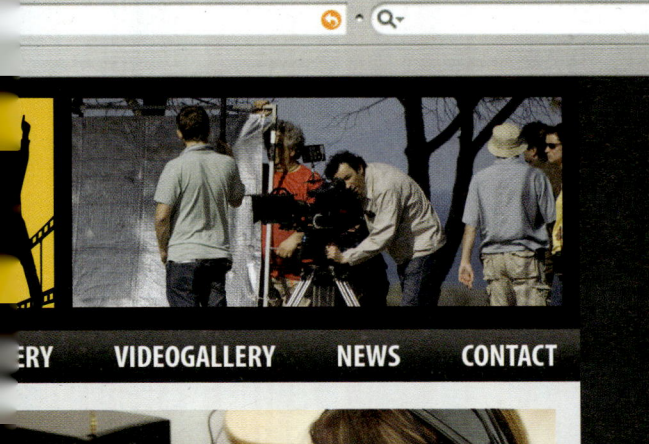

GRAMMAR

be

The LAC **is** an international school.
The classes **are** small and informal.
The LAC **isn't** only a British school.

Find more examples of the verb *to be* in the text. Underline the subject and the verb.

5 Underline the correct answer.
1 My friend John *is/are* in class 10B.
2 Ben and Jerry *aren't/isn't* blond, they're dark.
3 I'm *not/aren't* thin.
4 This CD *is/am* really cool!
5 You *aren't/isn't* Italian.
6 Redlands school *is/are* in Bristol.

GRAMMAR

have got

I**'ve got** a job.
We **haven't got** big classes.
Has it **got** a cinema?

Find more examples of *have got* in the text. Circle the subject and the verb.

6 Complete the sentences with the correct form of *have got*.
1 *I've got* a job. (✓)
2 A *Have you got* a friend? (you ?)
  B Yes, I *have* .
3 It _____ big classes. (✗)
4 A _____ a camera? (she ?)
  B No, she _____ .
5 We _____ courses for directors. (✗)
6 A _____ courses for actors? (they ?)
  B No, they _____ .

Write it!

7 Look at the items in ex. 1 and write what you have or haven't got.

I've got a mobile phone, a bus ticket… and… .
I haven't got a laptop, … or… .

Say it!

8 In pairs, ask and answer questions about what you've got for the new school year.

Have you got a laptop? Yes, I have./No, I haven't.

1

Are you Spanish?

1 🔊 **1.29** Listen and read. Where is Antonio from?

Antonio Hi, I'm Antonio. What's your name?
Michael Oh hello, I'm Michael. Where are you from? Are you Spanish?
Antonio No, I'm from Liverpool, but my mum's Italian.
Michael Italian? Where's she from?
Antonio Rome. What about you?
Michael I'm from Manchester.
Antonio Manchester, wow! You've got a great football team!
Michael Yeah, they're good. Have you got a place to stay, Antonio?
Antonio Yeah, I've got a room with a family. What about you?
Michael I've got an uncle and an aunt in London. And a cousin! Their house is huge – I've got a room there…
Antonio Great! By the way, this is Robyn. She's Scottish. Robyn, this is Michael.
Michael Hi, Robyn. Nice to meet you.
Robyn Hi! And this is Anna Harrison. She's from London. Her parents have got a B&B here.
Antonio B&B?
Robyn Yeah, you know, a 'Bed and Breakfast', the Victoria Palace Hotel.
Michael Anna, who's the man at the bar? Is he an actor?
Anna No, he isn't. He's Tony Harrison, he's my uncle, my dad's brother. He's the assistant director of the LAC. He's cool!
Tony Hello students, and welcome to the London Arts Centre…

2 Write the correct name after the sentence: Antonio, Michael, Robyn or Anna.

1 He's from Liverpool. _____
2 He's got a room with a family. _____
3 He's got an aunt in London. _____
4 She's got an uncle at the LAC. _____
5 She's got parents in London. _____
6 She's not English. _____
7 He's from Manchester. _____

3 In pairs, use the information from the dialogue to describe people and guess who they are.

A *He's got an Italian mum.*
B *Antonio.*
A *She's from Scotland.*
B *Robyn?*

FLASH FORWARD

Write about the people in your life. Where are they from?

I've got an uncle in Sydney.
My father is from Mumbai.

1

Vocabulary: The family

4 🔊 1.30 Look at the picture and complete the text with the words below. Be careful, there are two words more. Then listen and check your answers.

> ~~father~~ mother daughter brother
> sister son husband wife children

This is Julia Jolly the American actress. Her (1) _father_ Jack and her (2) _____ Pete Brad are actors too. She's got one (3) _____ James, he's 35, and she has got a (4) _____ , Marion, and a stepsister, Elizabeth. Julia and Pete have got five (5) _____ , a (6) _____ called Zanox, a (7) _____ called Zeeba, and twins called Nox and Venus. They've also got a baby girl called Shamana.

GRAMMAR

Wh- questions + be

What's **your** name?
Where **are** you from?

Find other examples of Wh- questions in the dialogue. Circle them.

5 Complete the sentences with the correct question word from the list.

> when what how where what

1 _____ 's your name?
2 _____ are the boys from?
3 _____ are you Diana? Fine thanks!
4 _____ 's your address?
5 _____ is your birthday?

GRAMMAR

Possessive adjectives

What's **your** name?
Their house is huge.

Find other examples of possessive adjectives in the dialogue. Underline them.

6 Complete the sentences with the correct possessive adjectives from the box.

> her my your its our his their

1 Is this _____ MP3 player, Mark?
2 These students haven't got _____ English books.
3 David is Helen's dad and Jane is _____ mum.
4 Mum, Neil and I haven't got _____ notebooks for school!
5 Where are _____ keys? They're not in my bag!
6 Graham's house is in Furness Street. _____ house is number 10.
7 The car is blue but _____ doors are red.

⚡ FLASHPOINT

We use the possessive *'s* or the apostrophe to indicate possession of something or to show the relationship between people.

It's Robert**'s** bag.
Jill, Jane and Judith**'s** mother is from Australia.
These are the girls**'** combs.

7 In pairs, ask and answer about Julia's family.

A *What's her father's name?*
B *His name's Jack.*

A *Who is Zanox?*
B *Zanox is her son.*

FUNCTIONS

Giving personal information

I'm Antonio.
I'm from Liverpool, but my mum's Italian.
I've got an uncle and an aunt in London. And a cousin!

8 Draw your family tree and write the names of your family members on it.

Say it!

9 Present yourself to the class. Give personal information and talk about your family.

My name's Ana, I'm from Barcelona. I'm 14 and I'm in class 1A. I've got one brother, Pablo but I haven't got a sister...

1 Vocabulary Workshop

Personal possessions

1 Complete the words for personal possessions.

1 com__
2 d__ary
3 MP__ pla__er
4 not__bo__k
5 la__to__
6 mob__l__ phone
7 tic__e__
8 ke__s
9 cas__ ca__d
10 ma__
11 p__ns
12 pen__ils
13 d__g__tal camera
14 wal__e__

2 Which words in exercise 1 are plural? Write a list.

The family

3 🔊 1.31 Complete Lucy's family tree with the words below. Then listen and check.

~~mother~~ father brother sister grandfather
grandmother uncle aunt cousin

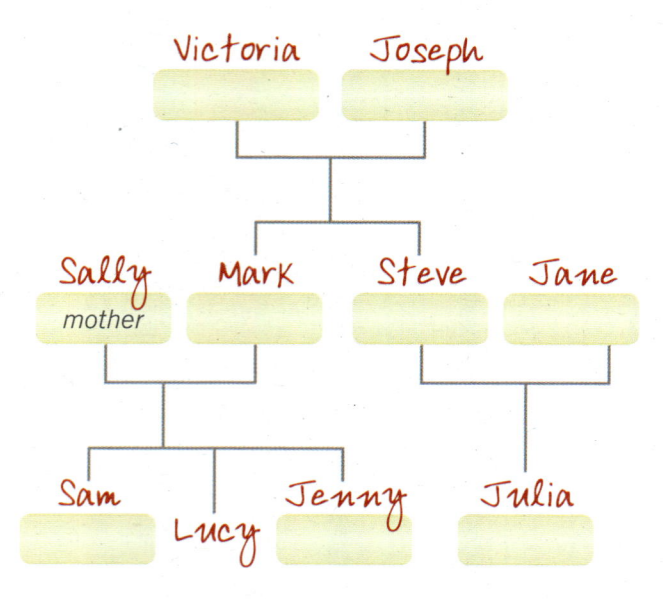

Victoria — Joseph

Sally — Mark   Steve — Jane

mother

Sam   Jenny   Julia
Lucy

4 Complete the sentences with the words below.

wife children son daughter
nieces nephew stepsisters stepbrother

1 Mr Smith has got two children, a _____, Tom, and a _____, Mary.
2 This is Mr Drake and his _____, Mrs Drake.
3 Cinderella has got two _____ in the story. They aren't nice!
4 My aunt Louise has got two _____, my sisters Anna and Clara.
5 John, this is my _____ Peter, my brother's son.
6 There are three _____ in our family now – me, my _____ George and my sister Helen.

5 Look at the words for family members again. Write them in the correct groups.

male — son
male or female — cousin
female — mother

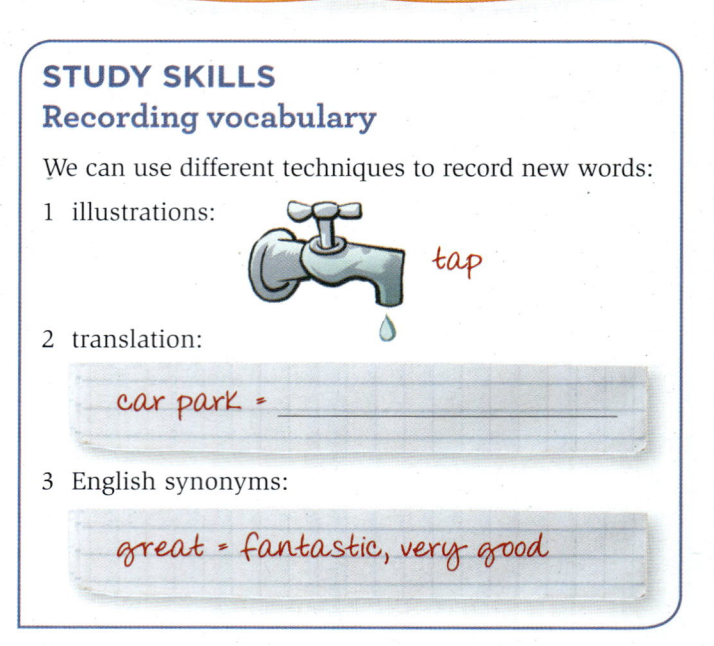

STUDY SKILLS
Recording vocabulary

We can use different techniques to record new words:

1 illustrations: tap

2 translation:
   car park = _____

3 English synonyms:
   great = fantastic, very good

6 Now record these new words. Use the techniques from the Study Skills box.

1 Draw a picture for:
   a camera   b clock   c double-decker bus
2 Translate:
   a assistant director   b parents   c by the way
3 Write a synonym for:
   a surname   b huge

Pronunciation: /h/

The letter *h* at the beginning of a word is generally aspirated.

7 🔊 1.32 Listen and repeat these words.

house his holiday her here have husband hotel

8 🔊 1.33 Listen and circle the word you hear, *a* or *b*?

1 a hit   b it
2 a hat   b at
3 a ear   b hear
4 a and   b hand
5 a hair   b air
6 a eat   b heat
7 a his   b is

9 🔊 1.34 Now listen, check your answers and repeat the words.

Flash on Grammar 1

be

Affirmative			Negative		
I	'm		I	'm not	
He/She/It	's	Scottish.	He/She/It	isn't	Scottish.
You/We/They	're		You/We/They	aren't	

Interrogative			Short answers
Am	I		
Is	he/she/it	Scottish?	Yes, I am./No, I'm not.
Are	we/you/they		

We use the verb *to be* to give information about:
- who we are/what we do: *I'm Antonio. I'm a student.*
- where we are: *I'm in London.*
- where we come from: *I'm from Manchester.*

Wh- questions + be

What's your name?   **Who are** our students?
Where's your bag?

📖 WB p. 4

1 Complete with the correct form of *be*.

1 '_Is_ this the train to Florence?'
  'Yes, it is.'
2 I _____ Portuguese, where _____ you from?
3 They are on holiday, they _____ at work.
4 'Are they brother and sister?' 'No, _____.'
5 'Is Pam English?' 'No, _____.'

2 Match the questions and answers.

1 What's your name?   a We're in London.
2 Where's your bag?   b It's in Brazil.
3 Where are the tickets?   c I'm from Ireland.
4 Where are you from?   d They're on the seat.
5 Where is São Paulo?   e It's on the chair.
6 Where are we?   f My name's Emma.

have got

Affirmative			Negative		
I/You/We/They	've got		I/You/We/They	haven't got	
He/She/It	's got	a car.	He/She/It	hasn't got	a car.

Interrogative			Short answers
Have	I/you/we/they		
Has	he/she/it	a car?	Yes, I have./No, I haven't.

We use *has/have got* to talk about:
- possession: *They've got a Bed and Breakfast.*
- family relations: *I've got a big family.*
- physical features: *I've got blue eyes.*

📖 WB p. 6

3 Rewrite these sentences in the negative or affirmative forms, like the examples.

1 I've got a cousin. *I haven't got a cousin.*
2 You haven't got a laptop. *You have got a laptop.*
3 I haven't got a passport. _____
4 They haven't got a daughter. _____
5 She's got a ticket. _____
6 They've got an MP3 player. _____

4 Complete the questions and short answers with *have/has got*.

1 _Has he got_ a dog? Yes, he _____.
2 _____ a laptop? No, we _____.
3 _____ a diary? No, she _____.
4 _____ a comb? Yes, I _____.
5 _____ three children? Yes, they _____.
6 _____ a map? No, he _____.

5 Complete the dialogue with *have/has got*.

Inspector (1) _____ you _____ a ticket, sir?
Man Yes, I (2) _____. Here it is.
Inspector I see. But this is a second class ticket.
Man Is it? Yes, you're right.
Inspector Yes, but this is a first class carriage.
Man Yes, it's nice.
Inspector But you (3) _____ a first class ticket, sir.
Man No, I haven't. What about this lady. (4) _____ a first class ticket?
Inspector Yes, she has.
Man Hmm. And these gentlemen. (5) _____ first-class tickets?
Inspector Yes, they have. (6) _____ all got first-class tickets, but you haven't!

Possessive adjectives

I	you	he	she	it	we	you	they
my	your	his	her	its	our	your	their

*This is **my** sister, Jenny.*
*Have you got **your** mobile phone?*

📖 WB p. 8

6 Complete the text with possessive adjectives.

Hi, I'm Paul and this is a photo of _____ two friends. The boy is _____ best friend. _____ name is Michael. The girl is _____ girlfriend. _____ name is Laura. The dog in the photo is a Labrador. _____ name is Seta.

29

1 Flash on Skills

London calling

Before you read

1 Match the photos above with the words.

1. ☐ pound coin
2. ☐ fish and chip shop
3. ☐ post box
4. ☐ hot and cold taps
5. ☐ pub
6. ☐ double-decker bus
7. ☐ black London taxi
8. ☐ deli

STUDY SKILLS
Reading for gist (1)

To understand the topic of a text look first at the title and any headings for the paragraphs or sections in it. Underline them, write them down in your notebook and think about what ideas connect them.

2 Look at Claudia's blog and the replies from other bloggers. Find and underline the title of the text and the bloggers' paragraphs. What is the topic of the text?

Title	
Paragraphs	
Topic	

3 How much do you know about London? Underline the correct option.

1. London is in the *south-east/south-west* of England.
2. London has got *100/1,000* theatres.
3. London has got a famous clock. It's called *Little/Big* Ben.
4. There are *14/4* million people in London.
5. The Tube is the name of the *airport/metro* system.
6. The name of the River in London is the *Mersey/Thames*.

Reading

4 Claudia, Antonio's cousin, is a student in London. Read her blog. Why is London great for Claudia?

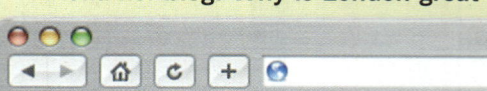

Claudia's blog

Why London is different

London's a great city and it's really special because there's a huge variety of things to do! It's got everything: culture, great museums and art galleries and theatres. Food is great – it's not just fish and chips, it's international! We've got food from all over the world and in Soho we've got great Italian delis!

As an Italian, I am very happy in London. There are 40,000 Italians in London, and 700 Italian students at London universities! We've got an 'Italians in London' website, check it out!

London's great for students like me – it's got clubs and cafes, it's got parks and museums and it's got a great music scene. Then the shopping in London is paradise! The city's got really fantastic shops from huge department stores like Harrods and Harvey Nicols, to expensive boutiques in Bond Street and Knightsbridge, to trendy fashion chains like Top Shop and H&M.

But London isn't just one city, it's a multicultural patchwork. There's African London, Asian London, Japanese London, Greek London, Polish London, Irish London, Italian London, Chinese London…

Post a reply.

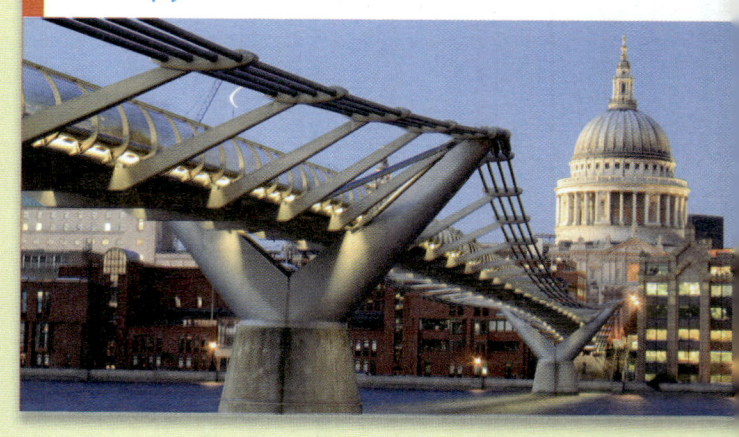

Culture 1

5 Now read the replies to Claudia's blog. Which of the things in the photos in exercise 1 do the bloggers mention? Write a list.

6 Read the statements and write T (true) or F (false), then correct the false sentences.

Claudia and other bloggers say...

1. English food is fantastic. ___
2. England's got 40,000 Italians. ___
3. Shopping in London isn't great. ___
4. The bathrooms in England are strange. ___
5. The UK has got the euro. ___
6. The UK hasn't got a monarch. ___

Recent Posts

Shops
Yeah, we've got the same shops in my country: Marks and Spencer, Zara, Mango, Gucci, Louis Vuitton... Shopping's the same everywhere.
Posted by Claire

Bathrooms
In England, why have they got two taps in the bathrooms: a hot tap and a cold tap? I'm from Spain and in my country we've got one tap for hot and cold water.
Posted by Pedro

Transport
Have they still got red double-decker buses in London?
Posted by Marta

Yes, they have, but now their name is 'Routemasters'. They've still got them because they're good for tourism!
Posted by Claudia

Money
Why haven't they got the Euro?
Posted by Mark

In the UK they've got the pound sterling. English people are very proud of the pound. It's a symbol of their identity.
Posted by Claudia

Monarchy
Why have they got a monarch, Queen Elizabeth?
Posted by Alex

Because they haven't got a President, the United Kingdom is a monarchy! I think the monarchy, with its palaces and everything, is great for tourism, like the red buses!
Posted by Claudia

Post your comment
Name
Email address

Listening

7 🔊 1.35 Listen to Claudia talking to her friend about food in London. Which five countries does she mention?

8 🔊 1.35 Listen again and answer the questions.

1. Which Italian food is very popular in Britain?
2. Write four Italian foods they've got in British supermarkets.
3. What kind of coffee have they got in British cafés now?

Writing

9 Complete this summary of the information in the blog with the words below.

> euros   city   supermarkets
> shops   monarch   buses   hot

London's a great city, it's the capital of England, in the United Kingdom. The (1) _____ are great, and the (2) _____ is fantastic. It's got everything: music, museums, theatres, clubs and pubs. The red double-decker (3) _____ are famous.
The UK is different from other countries: they've got pounds – not (4) _____, and they haven't got a President – they've got a (5) _____.
The bathroom taps are awful: one for cold and one for (6) _____ water.
The food in London is international and Italian food is very popular. They've got Italian, Chinese, Indian, Thai and Greek food in British (7) _____ now.

10 Now write a paragraph about a city in your country. Why is it special? Use these questions and exercise 9 to help you.

- Has it got good shops/good food/interesting or famous streets or monuments?
- Has it got theatres/music/museums, etc.?
- Why is your city different?

Speaking

11 In pairs, ask and answer questions to guess the city in your partner's paragraph.

A *Is it in this area?*
B *Yes it is.*
A *Has it got museums and art galleries?*
B *Yes, it has and it's got a famous stadium.*
A *Is it... ?*

31

2 Home Life

A day in the life of Rosa Barrios

Every month, we talk to people with interesting jobs. This month, we talk to Rosa Barrios from Barcelona.
In summertime we see lots of buskers in our cities. They play music and sing in the street for money, they dance, they paint. Rosa Barrios is 19 and she's Spanish but she lives in London, in a small bedsit in Camden. Rosa is a student and she does a very unusual job on Sundays.
'I work in the city centre. You see, I'm a living statue', she says, 'It's not easy but it's a very interesting job.'
Rosa gets up late at about 10 o'clock and she doesn't have breakfast. She has a shower then she gets dressed.
Does she wear special clothes for her job? 'Yes, I do. I've got a fantastic flamenco costume,' she says, 'With lots of different colours, or I wear my Tutankhamon costume.' Then she gets on her bike and she goes to work. 'I go to Leicester Square or Trafalgar Square, it depends. I find a good place and I don't move for hours, I usually stay there from midday to 3. Children stop and smile, or tease me.'
Do people give her money when she works? 'Yes,' says Rosa, 'It's a good job. I make a lot of money.'
What do her family and friends think? 'Well, my mum and dad don't like my job but my friends think I'm very brave. And when people see me on my bike in my flamenco costume they think, 'Wow!'

1 Match the photos to the words.
1 ☐ musician
2 ☐ dancer
3 ☐ busker
4 ☐ pavement artist

2 🔘 1.36 Listen and read the text. What is Rosa's job?

3 Choose the right answer.
1 Rosa is from…
 a ☐ England.
 b ☐ Spain.
 c ☐ France.
2 Rosa lives in…
 a ☐ Trafalgar Square.
 b ☐ Camden Town.
 c ☐ Leicester Square.
3 Rosa's job is…
 a ☐ interesting.
 b ☐ easy.
 c ☐ ordinary.
4 Rosa gets up…
 a ☐ at midday.
 b ☐ in the evening.
 c ☐ in the morning.
5 People say Rosa is…
 a ☐ brave.
 b ☐ strange.
 c ☐ exciting.

FLASH FORWARD

Which words describe Rosa's job? Put a tick (✓).

☐ unusual ☐ brave ☐ exciting
☐ difficult ☐ easy ☐ fantastic

GRAMMAR

Present simple

I **work** in the city centre.
She **lives** in London.

I **don't move** for hours.
She **doesn't have** breakfast.

Does she **wear** special clothes?
Yes, she does.
Do people **give** her money? Yes, they do.

Find more examples of the Present simple in the text. Underline them.

4 Complete the sentences with the correct form of the verbs below.

> go   work   paint   tell   play   get up

1 Buskers _____ music. (✓)
2 Rosa _____ at 7 o'clock. (✗)
3 My grandmother _____ stories. (✓)
4 Pavement artists _____ in studios. (✗)
5 I _____ in a school. I'm a teacher. (✓)
6 I _____ to school in New York. (✗)

5 In pairs, look at the sentences in ex. 4 and ask and answer questions.

A *Do buskers play music?*
B *Yes, they do.*

Vocabulary: Daily activities

6 Match the phrases to the pictures.

> go to bed   have a shower   ~~get up~~   watch TV
> start school   go home   have lunch   do homework

A  _____   B  _____   C *get up* (1 7.50)
D  _____   E  _____   F _____
G  _____   H _____ 

7 🔊 1.37 Listen to Mary's daily routine and put the activities in exercise 6 in the correct order.

FLASHPOINT

I get up at **ten to seven**.
They have dinner at **a quarter past 8**.
The train leaves at **6 p.m**.

8 🔊 1.37 Listen again and write the missing times.

Say it!

9 Work in pairs. Look at the pictures in ex. 6 again and ask and answer questions.

A *What time does Mary get up?*
B *She gets up at ten to eight.*

GRAMMAR

Prepositions of time

She gets up **at** 10 o'clock.
In summertime we see lots of buskers.
She does a very unusual job **on** Sundays.
I stay there **from** midday **to** 3.

10 Complete with *at*, *in*, *on*.

1 ___ Tuesday   4 ___ midnight
2 ___ winter   5 ___ the afternoon
3 ___ 6 o'clock   6 ___ weekends

FUNCTIONS

Talking about daily routines

What time do you watch TV?
I watch TV in the afternoon from 6 to 7.

Say it!

11 In pairs, say when you do the activities below.

> get up   have breakfast   have a shower
> have lunch   do homework   do sport
> have dinner   meet your friends

A *What time do you have a shower?*
B *I have a shower at 7.30 in the morning.*

Write it!

12 Write a text about your daily routine.

> *My typical day*
> *I get up at a quarter to seven.*
> *I have breakfast at...*

33

2

There's a sofa bed for friends

1 🔘 1.38 **Listen and read. Where does Anna live?**

Anna That's our B&B.
Antonio It's nice. Do you live there?
Anna Yes, I do. What about your house in London, is it nice?
Antonio Yes, it's great. I've got a bedsit in the attic with a double bed in it. Robyn's got a room there too.
Anna Cool! And does the landlady make your breakfast?
Robyn No, she doesn't, we make our breakfast!
Anna What about you, Mike? Have you got a big room in your aunt's house?
Michael Not really. It's a typical London house and my room's a bit small, but it's cosy. There's a bed in it and a desk, a big TV, a wardrobe for my clothes… Oh, and there's a sofa bed for friends, too!
Anna Wicked! And do you like London, Mike?
Michael I love London – there are hundreds of things to do! – but I don't go out in the evenings, I study! What about you, Anna?
Anna I work, so I get up early and go to bed late!
Antonio Wow! Have you got a job?
Anna Yes, I have. I work for my dad in the B&B. I want to do the course at the LAC, but there are… problems. Dad doesn't like the idea.
Antonio Bummer!

2 Complete the sentences with the correct names.

1 _____ lives in a B&B.
2 _____ has got a nice room.
3 _____ lives with Antonio.
4 _____ doesn't go out much.
5 _____ has got a job.

FLASH FORWARD

Where do you live? Have you got your own bedroom? Is it big or small? What's in it? Write about it.

I live in a house in Glasgow. I've got a big bedroom next to my parent's room. It's got …

Vocabulary:
Rooms and furniture

3 Look at the plan of the apartment. Write the names of the rooms using the words below.

> living room   bathroom   hall
> bedroom   kitchen   utility room

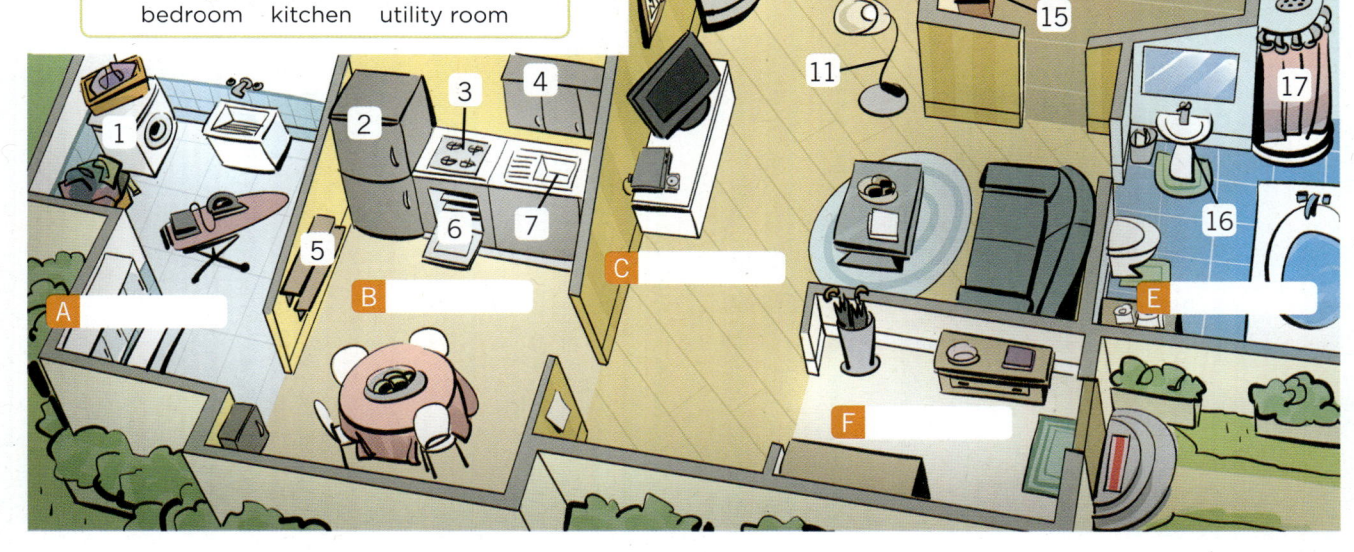

4 Find these things in the picture of the house. Write the numbers.

- ☐ oven
- ☐ carpet
- ☐ hob
- ☐ washing machine
- ☐ washbasin
- ☐ fireplace
- ☐ cupboard
- ☐ armchair
- ☐ fridge
- ☐ curtain
- ☐ sink
- ☐ lamp
- ☐ bookcase
- ☐ wardrobe
- ☐ shower
- ☐ bedside table
- ☐ shelves

5 🔊 1.39 Now listen, check your answers and repeat the words.

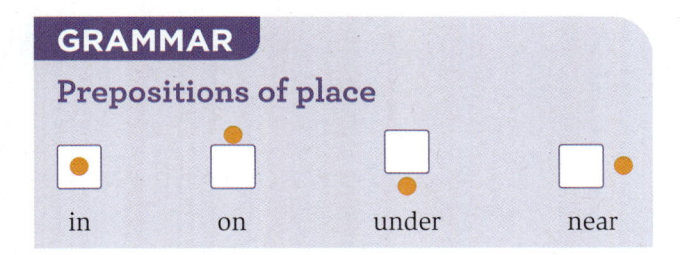

GRAMMAR
Prepositions of place

in   on   under   near

6 Look again at the picture in ex. 3 and complete the sentences with *in*, *on*, *under*, *near*.

1 The shelves are _____ the fridge.
2 The oven is _____ the hob.
3 The cushion is _____ the armchair.
4 The fireplace is _____ the living room.

! FLASHPOINT

There's a bed in it and a desk.
There are hundreds of things to do!

FUNCTIONS
Describing a room

What about your house in London?
I've got a bedsit in the attic with a double bed in it.

Have you got a big room?
No, my room's a bit small.

Say it!
7 Look at the photo of Robyn's bedsit. Describe it.

In her bedsit Robyn's got a bed and…

Write it!
8 Imagine your ideal home. Write a short text about it.

My ideal home has got twenty rooms. There's a big garden with a huge swimming pool…

2 Vocabulary Workshop

Rooms and furniture

1 Look at the photo of the house and find these things in it. Write the numbers.

☐ roof ☐ window ☐ hedge ☐ garden
☐ door ☐ garage ☐ chimney ☐ gate

2 🔊 1.40 Listen, check your answers and repeat the words.

STUDY SKILLS
Making a word web

A word web is a useful and very visual way to record new words. We use key words to group words into related sub-categories.

fridge — kitchen — Home — table

3 Copy the word web in your notebook and complete it with the words about home.

Verbs of daily routine

4 Write the verbs next to the activities.

get   have   do   go

1 _____ breakfast
2 _____ the shopping
3 _____ a snack
4 _____ home
5 _____ dinner
6 _____ to work
7 _____ homework
8 _____ sport
9 _____ dressed
10 _____ lunch
11 _____ to school
12 _____ up

Pronunciation: /s/ /ɪz/ /z/

In the Present simple, the third person -s or -es is pronounced:

- /s/ after the sounds /p/, /f/, /θ/, /t/, /k/
- /ɪz/ after the sounds /s/, /z/, /ʃ/, /ʒ/, /tʃ/, /dʒ/
- /z/ after all the others.

5 🔊 1.41 Listen and repeat the words.

S	IZ	Z
talks	washes	spends
_____	_____	_____
_____	_____	_____
_____	_____	_____

6 🔊 1.42 Listen and write the verbs in the correct column in the table in exercise 5.

watches looks studies takes prefers
knows brushes dresses makes buys

7 🔊 1.43 Now listen, check your answers and repeat the words.

Spoken English

In spoken, colloquial English, we use expressions like *Wicked!*, *Cool!*, *Wow!* to express surprise or delight in something positive. We use *Bummer!* to express empathy about something negative.

A *Robyn's got a room there too.*
B **Cool!**

A *There's a sofa bed for friends too!*
B **Wicked!**

A *Dad doesn't like the idea.*
B **Bummer!**

8 Reply to these statements. Use expressions from the box.

1 A Nancy has got a new iPhone.
  B _____ !
2 A My cat has got two tails.
  B _____ !
3 A I haven't got my wallet!
  B _____ !
4 A We've got chocolate ice cream for dessert.
  B _____ !

Flash on Grammar 2

Present simple

Affirmative		Negative	
I/You/We/They	work.	I/You/We/They	don't work.
He/She/It	works.	He/She/It	doesn't work.

Interrogative			Short answers
Do	I/you/we/they	work?	Yes, I do./No, I don't.
Does	he/she/it	work?	Yes, he does./No, he doesn't.

We use the Present simple to talk about habits, routine actions and permanent situations.

*She **gets up** early.* *They **work** in a hotel.*

Spelling rules

In the third person singular we add *-es* if the verb ends in *-o, -s, -ss, -sh, -ch, -x, -z.*
If the verb ends in a *consonant + -y*, the *-y* becomes *-i* and we add *-es.*

do → do**es**   watch → watch**es**   study → stud**ies**

📖 WB p. 16

1 Underline the correct answer.

1. I *play/plays* the piano.
2. Britney *sing/sings* pop songs.
3. Our teacher *tell/tells* great stories.
4. De Niro and Pacino *work/works* in the USA.
5. George Clooney *likes/like* Italy.
6. We *go/goes* out on Saturday with friends.

2 Make these sentences negative.

1. My mum paints pictures.
   My mum doesn't paint pictures.
2. My friend smiles a lot.
3. My friends laugh a lot.
4. I like music.
5. My friends and I go to the opera.
6. I work on Saturday.

3 Make questions from the sentences in exercise 2, then write answers that are true for you.

1. *Does my mum paint pictures?*
   No she doesn't./Yes, she does.

4 Complete the interview with Rosa Barrios' mother.

A Mrs Barrios, (1) _do_ you come from Spain?
B Yes, I (2) _____ .
A I see. And do you (3) _____ in London now?
B No, I (4) _____ . I live in Granada.
A And what (5) _____ your daughter do?
B She (6) _____ a living statue.
A (7) _____ you and Mr Barrios like Rosa's job?
B No, we (8) _____ . But Rosa loves her job and we love Rosa.

5 Rewrite the text below, make it true for you.

Research says that British teenagers spend about eight or nine hours in bed on a typical day at the weekend! Teenagers have got about six hours of free time a day and they spend three hours on their homework, about an hour shopping and they talk, or send sms messages, for forty-five minutes a day on their mobile phones!

I spend nine hours in bed…

Prepositions of time

at	at five o'clock, at lunch, at Easter
in	in five minutes, in the morning, in May, in spring, in 2011
on	on Thursday, on the 25th of October, on Christmas Day
from… to	from 9 a.m. to 1 p.m., from April to June, from 2008 to 2010

📖 WB p. 16

6 Complete the sentences with the correct preposition: *in, on, at, from… to*.

1. Halloween is ____ the 31st of October.
2. They play football ____ the evening in the park.
3. We are never cold at our mountain house ____ winter.
4. His father was born ____ 1965.
5. We've got Geography ____ 2 ____ 3 p.m.
6. The party starts ____ dinnertime.

Prepositions of place

in	in the box, in the north, in Italy
on	on the table, on the wall
near	near the sofa
under	under the bed

📖 WB p. 17

7 Think about your bedroom. Where are these things? Write sentences with *in, on, near* or *under*.

1. Where is the bed?
2. Where is the window?
3. Where is the wardrobe?
4. Where is the lamp?
5. Where are your books or DVDs?
6. Where are your clothes?

37

2 Flash on Skills

A land and its people

Before you read

1 Match these words with the correct pictures.

1. ☐ seal   3. ☐ whale   5. ☐ snowmobile
2. ☐ fish   4. ☐ sledge

STUDY SKILLS
Identifying text types

To help you identify text types look carefully at these characteristics:

- the layout of the text on the page – are there titles, short or long paragraphs, lists of words, highlighted words, captions, speech balloons?
- the visual material with the text – are there photographs, drawings, graphs or tables?

2 Look at the text on the right. Think about the characteristics in the Study Skills box. What type of text is it? (✓)

☐ a diary   ☐ a brochure
☐ an encyclopedia ☐ a cartoon story

3 How much do you know about the Inuit? Write T (true) or F (false).

1. They live in Russia. ___
2. They live in igloos. ___
3. They kiss with their noses. ___
4. They only eat vegetables. ___
5. They've got big families. ___

Reading

4 Now read the text and check your answers to exercise 3.

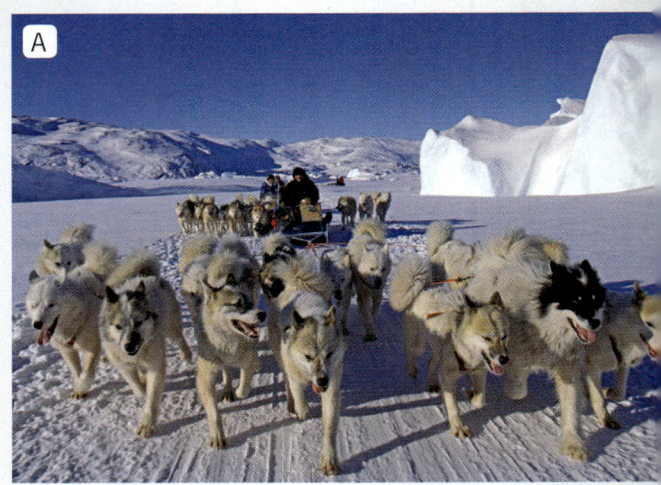

1 ☐ The Inuit live in the Arctic region of Greenland, Canada and Siberia. They live in large family groups – aunts, uncles, grandparents and cousins – and the men and women have different jobs in their society, for example men build houses and go fishing, and women cook, look after children and make clothes.

2 ☐ Today the Inuit go shopping for their food, but traditionally they eat mainly fish, whales and seals. They use all parts of the animals they catch. They make clothes from sealskins to protect them from the cold, and they use oil from whales and seals for light and heat.

CLIL 2

5 Read the text again and match the paragraphs to the photographs.

6 Answer the questions.
1. Where do the Inuit come from?
2. What jobs do a) men do and b) women do, in their society?
3. What do they use seals, whales and fish for?
4. What is an igloo?
5. How do the Inuit travel today?

Listening

7 🔊 1.44 Listen to the interview with an Inuit boy, Tarbak. Where does he live in the summer? And in the winter?

8 🔊 1.44 Listen again. Complete the table about Tarbak's daily life.

morning	
afternoon	
evening	

Writing

9 Complete this summary of the text with the correct words.

The Inuit live in the Arctic. They (1) _____ in large family groups. Men and women have different (2) _____ , for example, men (3) _____ houses and go fishing, women (4) _____ and (5) _____ children. Today the Inuit buy their (6) _____ in shops but traditional food for the Inuit is (7) _____ and (8) _____ . They use all the parts of the (9) _____ they catch.
The Inuit usually live in (10) _____ , but some use traditional igloos for fishing trips in winter. For transport, they don't use only dogs and sledges now, they also have (11) _____ .

Speaking

10 Make notes of things in Inuit life which are similar to/different from life in your country. Talk about the differences and similarities.

Similar	Different
They eat fish.	They eat seals.

In England we eat fish but we don't eat seals!

C

D

E

3 ☐ The word igloo is an Inuit word for house. People think that the Inuit all live in igloos but in fact today they usually live in towns: igloos are winter shelters, they sometimes use them when they go fishing.

4 ☐ The Inuit don't use only traditional dogs and sledges for transport nowadays, many of them have got snowmobiles. But sometimes they travel by dog sledge when the snowmobiles are too heavy for the ice.

5 ☐ And, by the way, the Inuit don't really kiss with their noses but Inuit mothers sometimes touch their children's faces with their noses.

39

1 Flashback

GRAMMAR

be

1 Complete the gaps with the correct form of the verb *to be*.

0 She _is_ Chinese. She comes from Shanghai.
1 I _____ French. I'm from France.
2 You _____ Italian. You're from Germany.
3 He _____ from Ireland. He's Irish.
4 She's a teacher. She _____ a director.
5 The school is in London. It _____ in New York.
6 We _____ students at the Arts Centre. We aren't teachers.
7 They _____ Canadian. They're English.
8 She isn't in London. She _____ in Madrid now.
9 We _____ from Liverpool. We're from Manchester.
10 You're not a teacher. You _____ a student.

[10]

2 Complete these questions and answers with one or two words.

0 _Are you_ from London? Yes, I am.
1 _____ I late for school? Yes, you are.
2 _____ from France? No, I'm not.
3 _____ a doctor? No, he isn't.
4 _____ a teacher? Yes, she is.
5 Are these keys yours? Yes, _____ .
6 Is the mobile phone new? No, it _____ .
7 _____ Jack? No, I'm not.
8 Are _____ brother and sister? Yes, they are.
9 Is he your husband? No, _____ isn't.
10 _____ actors? No, they aren't.

[10]

have got

3 Complete the sentences with the correct form of *has/have got*. Use short forms.

0 I _haven't got_ a diary. (✗)
1 They _____ tickets. (✓)
2 My brother _____ a laptop. (✗)
3 You _____ a digital camera. (✓)
4 We _____ keys. (✗)
5 I _____ a passport. (✓)
6 She _____ a notebook. (✓)
7 Hannah and Tony _____ got a map. (✗)
8 My mum and dad _____ a cash card. (✓)
9 The students _____ a video camera. (✗)
10 The school _____ two directors. (✓)

[10]

4 Complete the questions and short answers.

0 Have you got a cold? Yes, I _have_ .
1 Have we got homework today? Yes, we _____ .
2 _____ you got a bicycle? No, I haven't.
3 _____ she got a daughter? No, she hasn't.
4 Have they got an MP3 player? Yes, they _____ .
5 Has the dog got a name? No, it _____ .
6 _____ I got a good mark? Yes, you have.

[6]

Possessive adjectives

5 Complete the sentences with the correct possessive adjectives.

| her | my | your | its | our | ~~his~~ | their |

0 My brother is married. _His_ wife is very nice.
1 This is _____ brother, John. I haven't got a sister.
2 Jerry is Helen's dog and Tom is _____ cat.
3 Lisa and Sue haven't got _____ books today.
4 _____ school is very good – we like it.
5 Italy is a great country. _____ museums are famous.
6 A Paul, is this _____ book?
   B Yes, it is. Thank you.

[6]

Present simple

6 Complete the sentences. Use the correct form of the verbs below.

| teach | cost | have | speak | get | ~~have~~ | read |

0 I _have_ a shower at 7.30 every morning.
1 Every day I _____ up at the same time.
2 She _____ very good English.
3 A lot of English people _____ a newspaper when they are on the train.
4 Nick and Miriam _____ lunch at 2 o'clock.
5 iPhones are expensive; they _____ a lot of money.
6 He's a great teacher; he _____ Maths.

[6]

7 Complete these sentences with the negative or positive form of the verbs in brackets.

0 She _doesn't get up_ early. (get up ✗)
1 She _____ in a hotel. (work ✓)
2 They _____ classical music. (like ✗)
3 Rosa and her friend _____ shopping in Camden. (go ✓)
4 We _____ a big breakfast. (have ✓)
5 He _____ special clothes. (wear ✗)
6 This mobile phone _____ . (work ✗)

[6]

40

Flashback 1 2

Prepositions of time

8 Complete with *at*, *in*, *on*.

0 She has a shower *in* the morning.
1 We don't go to school ___ Saturday.
2 We go out ___ weekends.
3 It is hot in Lisbon ___ summer.
4 She goes to bed ___ midnight.
5 I do my homework ___ the afternoon.

[5]

Prepositions of place

9 Complete with *in*, *on*, *under*, *near*.

0 Mum is *in* the bedroom.
1 Our house is _____ the school.
2 The food is _____ the table.
3 The dog is _____ the table.
4 The fireplace is _____ the living room.
5 The fridge is _____ the oven.

[5]

Round up!

10 Complete the gaps with one word.

A What's (0) *your* name?
B My name's Silvia Rossi.
A Are (1) _____ Spanish?
B Well, my mum's Spanish but (2) _____ dad's from Italy.
A (3) _____ is your dad from in Italy?
B Milan. But I've (4) _____ an aunt and uncle in Rome.
A I see. Have you got relatives (5) _____ Spain?
B Yes, my grandparents (6) _____ in Barcelona.
A (7) _____ you go to Spain?
B Yes, we go (8) _____ the summer. I've got a lot of friends.
A (9) _____ your dad speak Spanish?
B Yes, he does.
A And does your mum (10) _____ Italian?
B Yes, we all speak Spanish and Italian.

[10]

VOCABULARY
Personal possessions

11 Find the personal possessions in these jumbled words.

0 bocm   c*omb*
1 porpasst   p_____
2 llwate   w_____
3 shcacrda   c_____
4 aiyrd   d_____
5 nbooteok   n_____
6 tiectk   t_____

[6]

The family

12 Complete the chart with the missing words.

Male	Female
father	(0) *mother*
(1) _____	daughter
brother	(2) _____
(3) _____	grandmother
stepbrother	(4) _____
(5) _____	wife
uncle	(6) _____
(7) _____	cousin

[7]

FUNCTIONS
Giving personal information

13 Complete the dialogue with one or two words in each gap.

A (0) *What's* your name?
B My name (1) _____ Helen Phillips.
A (2) _____ are you from?
B I'm (3) _____ Birmingham.
A (4) _____ 's Birmingham?
B (5) _____ in England.
A Where's your passport?
B It (6) _____ in my bag.
A (7) _____ 's your job?
B I'm an actress.

[7]

Describing a room

14 Write the word for each picture in this description.

In my bedroom I've got a (0) *bed* and an (1) _____ . There's a table and on the table there's a (2) _____ and a (3) _____ . There's a fireplace and a (4) _____ for my clothes. In the bathroom, there's a shower and a (5) _____ . In the kitchen, there's an oven and a (6) _____ .

[6]

Total: 100

41

3 My Ideal Holiday

Robbie's blog

1 Do you know these words for holiday activities? Complete the expressions under the pictures.

1 s___m

2 vi__it mon__ments

3 m__ke new frie__ds

4 s__nbath__

2 🔊 1.45 Listen and read Robbie's blog. What does he think about study camp holidays? Put a tick (✓).

a ☐ They're fun.   b ☐ They're educational.   c ☐ They're not interesting.

HOME | ABOUT | SUBSCRIBE VIA RSS / SUBSCRIBE VIA EMAIL | Enter name | Enter email | SUBSCRIBE

Cool holidays

Most kids always go on holiday with their families. They go to a hotel or an apartment, they visit monuments on 'educational' trips and they sometimes go to eat in restaurants. Okay, maybe young kids enjoy all that but for a teenager, how often do you hear them say, 'It's soooo boring!'?!

I'm 16 now and I don't like going on holiday with my parents every year. I want to go with my friends sometimes; I like doing fun things – teenage things! My parents always say, 'No Robbie, come with us to Cornwall,' (they go to Cornwall every year!). But this year is different! I've got some money from my Saturday job and I've got a plan – a study camp holiday in the USA!

The camp is in Vermont and the programme looks fantastic! In the morning there are study courses in Art, Music and Drama (okay, I don't usually like lessons but I don't mind these courses – they're cool!). In the afternoon, there are outdoor activities – you play sports or go rafting, canoeing, wind-surfing... (I love water sports!), sometimes you feel lazy, so you just sunbathe and swim in the lake and stuff. They often organize camping trips too – you go by horse and sleep in tents in the forest! Wicked!

The accommodation is similar to a youth hostel – you sleep in a big room and everyone helps to cook the meals and clean up. The students come from all over the world – it's great! – I love meeting people from other countries and making new friends...

Connect with me

7 comments

---

3 Answer the questions.

1 Where does Robbie want to go on holiday?
2 What type of holiday is it?
3 Write three things students do in the mornings at the camp.
4 Write the outdoor activities at the camp.
5 Where do the students sleep at the camp?
6 Where are the students from?

3

GRAMMAR
Adverbs of frequency

How often do you hear them say…?
Most kids **always** go on holiday with their families.
They **sometimes** go to eat in a restaurant.

0%					100%
never	hardly ever	sometimes	often	usually	always

Find more examples of adverbs of frequency in the text. Underline them.

4 Put an adverb of frequency in these sentences to make them true for you.

1. I _often_ play sports after school.
2. My parents _____ go on holiday to Spain.
3. How _____ do you go to the sea?
4. On holiday, I _____ go swimming.
5. At home, I _____ get up early.
6. At weekends, I _____ go to bed late.

Vocabulary: Holiday accommodation

5 🔘 1.46 Write the words under the photos, then listen and check.

> hotel   bed and breakfast   youth hostel
> camper   tent   apartment

1 _____   2 _____

3 _____   4 _____

5 _____   6 _____

Say it!
6 Talk about the types of accommodation where your family stays on holiday.

We often stay in a bed and breakfast in Valencia. We never stay in a tent…

FUNCTIONS
Expressing preferences

I **love** meeting people from other countries.
I **don't** usually **like** lessons.
I **don't mind** these courses.

7 Complete these mini-dialogues with expressions from the functions box.

1. A Do you like coffee?
   B Well, I _____ like it, but this coffee is delicious!
2. A Do you like the LAC, Judy?
   B Yes, I do. There are students from all over the world and I _____ meeting new people!
3. A I like your jeans. Do you always wear jeans to parties, Susie?
   B No, I don't. I _____ jeans but I prefer skirts really.

Say it!
8 What do you like doing on your holiday? Ask and answer questions using the expressions from the functions box and the *-ing* form.

> do homework   play sports   sleep in the sun
> eat ice cream   get up late   make new friends
> visit monuments   go on picnics   swim in the sea

A *Do you like doing homework on holiday?*
B *No, I don't! I never do homework on holiday!*

A *Do you enjoy swimming in the sea?*
B *Yes, but I prefer swimming in the pool.*

Write it!
9 Write a text about your favourite type of holiday. Use Robbie's blog as a model.

> I usually go on holiday with my parents. I like going to the countryside and I enjoy cycling with my mum.

43

3

I hate cycling in traffic!

1 🔊 **1.47** Look at the photograph. Where are the friends? What type of transport departs from there? Then listen and read to check your answers.

Michael Hi, Robyn. You're late!
Robyn Yeah, the Tube's really crowded now – I can't stand it! And the trains are often late.
Michael Yeah, it's a real pain… I prefer the bus.
Antonio Really? But the buses are usually late too! I always go by bike!
Robyn Oh, no! You know me – I hate cycling in traffic! Where's Anna, Mike? I don't see her…
Michael She's late too – it's this terrible rain! She wants to meet us in Leicester Square.
Robyn Does she? How do you get to Leicester Square from here?
Michael I think it's on the Piccadilly line. Let's ask…

Michael Excuse me, do the trains on this line stop at Leicester Square?
Woman No, they don't, dear. This is the Central line. For Leicester Square take the Central line for three stops, then change at Holborn station. Look.
Michael Holborn, okay…
Woman At Holborn you take the Piccadilly line – it's the blue line.
Michael Does the Piccadilly train go straight to Leicester Square?
Woman Yes, it does. It's two stops.
Michael That's great, thanks very much.
Woman You're welcome.

2 Read the statements and write T (true) or F (false).

1. Robyn comes to the station by bicycle. ___
2. She likes cycling in London. ___
3. Anna is at the Underground station, too. ___
4. This station is on the Central line. ___
5. The Central line doesn't go to Holborn. ___
6. The woman tells Michael to change at Piccadilly. ___
7. The Piccadilly train goes directly to their destination. ___
8. Leicester Square is three stops from where the friends are. ___

FLASH FORWARD

Correct the false sentences in ex. 2.

44

3

GRAMMAR

Object pronouns

You know **me** – I hate cycling in traffic!
She wants to meet **us** in Leicester Square.

Find more examples of object pronouns in the text. Underline them.

3 Match the object pronouns to the words they represent.

1 She always takes it with her.
2 I enjoy meeting them.
3 He loves her.
4 I see him.
5 No, I don't like it.

a new people
b her MP3 player
c Peter
d Sharon
e your new mobile phone

Vocabulary: Transport

4 🔊 **1.48** Complete the words for types of transport under the pictures. Then listen and check your answers.

1 tr __ __ n
2 bi __ e
3 c __ r
4 mo __ orbi __ e 
5 bu __ 
6 sh __ p 
7 t __ x __ 
8 v __ n 
9 fe __ r __ 

⚠ FLASHPOINT

Do you always **take the train**?
I sometimes **go by bike** to school.

Say it!

5 How do you travel to school? Talk about the means of transport that you take.

I usually go to school by car with my dad but sometimes I take the bus.

FUNCTIONS

Asking for travel information

Excuse me, does this bus stop at the zoo?
Yes, the zoo is two stops from here.

Does the number 15 bus go to the centre?
No, it doesn't.

How do you get to Westminster from here?
Take the Central line for three stops.

⚠ FLASHPOINT

Does this train **go to** Oxford?
Does the number 4 bus **stop at** the Odeon cinema?

Say it!

6 🔊 **1.49** In pairs, listen and repeat the dialogues. Then substitute the words in blue for places in your town to make new dialogues.

1 A Does this train go to London?
  B Yes, it does.
  A Does it stop at York?
  B No, it doesn't.

2 A Excuse me, do all these buses go to the city centre?
  B No, they don't. You want the 32 or the 11.
  A Okay, thanks.

3 A How do you get to the railway station from here?
  B Take the number 25 bus for four stops. It's opposite the Grand Hotel.

Write it!

7 Write a quiz about transport. Use the prompts below.

1 you / travel / to school / usually?
2 your parents / go to work / usually?
3 your family / has got / one or two cars?
4 you / have got / a bicycle?
5 how often / you / use / a bus?
6 how often / you / travel / by bicycle?

8 Give your quiz to five classmates to complete. Look at their answers and write a summary of the results.

Three people go to school by bus. One person goes to school by car...

3 Vocabulary Workshop

Holiday activities

1 Which of these activities do you do on holiday and which every day? Write them in the correct groups. Which activities can you write in both groups?

> playing sports   chatting to friends online
> sleeping   making new friends   listening to music
> swimming   eating in restaurants
> playing computer games   watching television
> doing homework   sunbathing   reading

holiday activities   everyday activities

2 In pairs, answer the questions about your favourite activities.
1 Which of these activities do you like/not like doing on holiday?
2 Which of the activities do you do at the weekend?
3 How often do you do them?

Transport

3 Read these words and translate them into your own language.
1 coach   _____
2 lorry   _____
3 helicopter   _____
4 scooter   _____
5 airplane   _____
6 the Underground   _____

4 In pairs, complete the table with the words for transport. You can use some words twice.

> train   bicycle   car   motorbike   bus   ship
> taxi   van   ferry   coach   lorry   helicopter
> scooter   airplane   the Underground

	travels in the air	travels in the water	travels on land
2 wheels			
4 wheels			a car
4-8 wheels			
No wheels			

STUDY SKILLS
Writing word definitions

Another technique which can help you remember new words is to make a list, then write definitions. Use a bilingual dictionary to check you understand the meaning in your own language, then write a definition for the word in simple English.

> *swim:* a sport you do in the water.
> *sunbathe:* an activity you do on holiday, to relax in the sun.

Holiday accommodation

5 Match the words to their definitions.
1 ☐ bed and breakfast
2 ☐ camper
3 ☐ self-catering apartment

a A type of van with accommodation inside it, you cook meals in it.
b A private house in a holiday location.
c A private house with extra rooms, you sleep and have breakfast in it.

6 Check the meanings of the words below, then write definitions for them.

> tent   youth hostel   resort

Pronunciation: /ŋ/

The suffix *-ing* which forms the gerund is pronounced and represented by the phoneme /ŋ/.

7 🔊 1.50 Listen and repeat the words and expressions in the table.

/ŋ/	/n/
thing, wing, bang, swimming, playing, _____	thin, win, ban, swim in, play in, _____

8 🔊 1.51 Listen and write these words in the correct columns in the table in exercise 7.

> ring   relax in   stink   lying   Ron
> van   relaxing   rang   wrong   lie in

9 🔊 1.52 Now listen, check your answers and repeat the words.

Flash on Grammar 3

Adverbs of frequency

We use adverbs of frequency to say how often an action is carried out. In general, they go after the subject and before the majority of verbs.
He **always** arrives early.

We use adverbs of frequency after the verb *to be*.
They are **usually** busy.

Sometimes can be used at the beginning or at the end of a sentence.

To specify how many times an action is repeated, we use expressions like:
every day/week/month...
once/twice... a day/a week/a month,
but *three times* a day/month/year...

These expressions usually go at the end of the sentence.
He plays tennis **every Thursday**.

To ask questions about frequency we use
How often...?
How often does she play golf?

📖 WB p. 24

1 Put the adverbs in the correct position.

| often | usually | hardly ever | never | sometimes |

0%   100%
____   ____   ____   ____   ____   always

2 Put an arrow where the adverbs go in the sentences.

1 I ↓ go to school on foot. (usually)
2 I take the bus. (every day)
3 She goes swimming. (sometimes)
4 Holidays are expensive. (often)
5 My parents go to the same hotel. (every year)
6 We watch TV. (always, in the evening)

3 Put these words in the correct order to make sentences.

1 the bus / take / I / never
   I never take the bus.
2 listens to / she / her MP3 / always
   _____
3 travel / bike / usually / they / by
   _____
4 homework / we / every / day / do
   _____
5 in the summer / usually / is / he / on holiday
   _____
6 Mum and Dad / on Saturday / often / the cinema / go to
   _____

Verbs of preference + -ing

We use the following verbs to express tastes and preferences: *like, love, enjoy, prefer, don't mind, hate, can't stand*.

They are usually followed by a verb in the *-ing* form or by a noun.
I like **going** on holiday.
I hate **maths**.

📖 WB p. 24

4 Write sentences using the prompts.

1 my brother / love / swim
   My brother loves swimming.
2 Sally / not like / pizza
3 my parents / hate / watch / horror films
4 my cat / hate / go out / in the rain
5 lady Gray / enjoy / listen / classical music?
6 we / not mind / stay in / tonight

5 Make sentences using the verbs of preference and the expressions in the box.

| buy clothes   go to the dentist |
| play computer games   get up early |
| speak English   do homework   sunbathe |

I love sunbathing.

Object pronouns

I	you	he	she	it	we	you	they
me	you	him	her	it	us	you	them

Object pronouns substitute nouns.
We use them after a verb or a preposition.

I enjoy swimming. → I enjoy **it**.
I don't mind going out with my parents. → I don't mind going out with **them**.

📖 WB p. 25

6 Complete the sentences with the correct object pronoun.

1 Graham is our neighbour. We live near _____ .
2 Where are my keys? Louise has got _____ .
3 Is Katie that girl with long, red hair? No, that's not _____ .
4 Where is my comb? The baby has got _____ .
5 I'm sure Sally likes _____ . She calls my mobile phone every day!
6 Mum! Dad! There's a letter for _____ from my teacher.

47

3 Flash on Skills

Island adventures

Before you read

1 Look at the covers of famous books below. Do you know any of these stories? Which covers do you like? Which cover makes you want to read the book?

2 Match the literary genres with the book covers.
- ☐ science fiction
- ☐ biography
- ☐ fantasy
- ☐ horror
- ☐ adventure
- ☐ thriller
- ☐ crime
- ☐ travel
- ☐ humour
- ☐ romance

3 What genre of books do you think these sentences come from? Choose from the literary genres in exercise 2.
1. 'My first memory is of my grandmother's house in Cornwall.'
2. 'She looks into his eyes and suddenly Emily knows their love is real.'
3. 'This is a gadget we're developing for you, Bond – it's a pen with a camera inside.'
4. 'They say vampires are nocturnal creatures.'
5. 'The alien spaceship emitted a strange green light.'
6. 'You're under arrest, Capone.'

Reading

4 Read the plot summaries of two famous children's books. Which literary genre do they come from?

Treasure Island

Young Jim Hawkins finds a pirate's map of an island. Jim takes the map to his friends Squire Trelawney and Doctor Livesey. It is a treasure map – the old pirate Captain Flint's gold! They decide to go and look for the treasure. The Squire buys a ship, the 'Hispaniola', and he finds some sailors for it. One of them is a strange cook with one leg, a man called Long John Silver.

The night before they reach Treasure Island Jim hears Long John Silver and some of the sailors talking about a plot to kill Trelawney and Livesey. He realises that Silver and these sailors are really pirates and know about Captain Flint's treasure. Jim tells the Captain of the Hispaniola about the evil plans and he sends the pirates to the island to decide what to do. Jim follows them in secret and hides in the trees. Ben Gunn, a crazy old pirate, lives on the island and he promises to help Jim and his friends. Now a great story of danger, bravery and adventure begins…

STUDY SKILLS
Identifying literary genres

Identifying what genre it is helps us understand the topic and general sense of a literary text. First, look at the words in the title and any illustrations to find clues to the genre, then look for key words in the text which are related to the title topic and confirm your idea.

Literature 3

5 Read the sentences below and mark the correct answer *a*, *b*, or *c*.

1. The map Jim finds is of…
   a some treasure. b the Underground. c an island.
2. The cook on the ship is really…
   a the author. b a pirate. c a boy.
3. Long John Silver and the sailors want to kill…
   a Jim. b Ben Gunn. c Jim's friends.
4. At first the children on the island are…
   a relaxed. b depressed. c happy.
5. The big boys want to hunt…
   a fish. b the little boys. c animals.
6. The little boys are afraid of…
   a the night. b the animals. c the big boys.

Lord of the Flies

An airplane crashes on a desert island and a group of school boys are the only survivors. At first they are happy there – there aren't any adults, they are free, the island is a paradise for them. While they wait for a ship to find them, they create their own 'micro-society' and split into two groups.

One group makes Ralph their 'chief', and he organises shelter and fire and collects food. Jack, the head of the other group, takes his boys hunting for wild pigs. Jack and Ralph become rivals. Jack's hunters become savage, Ralph's group is more civilized. The little boys in Ralph's group become afraid of the big boys in Jack's as they start to look for new victims to hunt. The growing hostility between the two groups leads to a frightening climax.

6 Read the summaries and answer these questions.

1. Where are the stories set?
   _____
2. Who are the main characters?
   _____
3. What are they about?
   _____

Listening

7 🔊 1.53 Listen to two friends talking about books. Complete the chart about the books they mention.

	author	title	genre
Martin	Paul Theroux		
Jill			

8 What is similar about the books the two friends like?

9 🔊 1.53 Listen again. Which of the questions from exercise 6 do you hear in the dialogue? Write them.

Writing

10 Think about an adventure or travel story you know (or another type of story, if you prefer). Prepare a short summary of the story. Use the chart from exercise 7 and the questions from exercise 6 to help you. Think about these points too.

- How does the story start and end?
- What do the characters do in the story?
- Who do they meet?
- What are the main events in the story?

Speaking

11 Work in pairs. Tell him/her about your story, then swap roles.

My favourite travel story is… by…

12 Report back to the class about your partner's story. Can you remember everything he/she said?

Richard's favourite story isn't a travel story, it's an adventure story. It's called…

49

4 What's in Fashion?

Trends

TREND INTERVIEW

In this week's *Trend* interview, we ask teenagers on the streets of Britain, 'What are you wearing today – and why?'

Trend Jessica, you're wearing very trendy clothes – jeans, a red hoodie, a vest top and trainers. What a cool look! Why do you like these clothes?

Jessica Well, I'm wearing jeans because they're comfortable and I'm wearing this top because it's skater-style.

Trend Johnny, you're wearing skateboarding clothes too, right?

Johnny Yeah, that's right. Jessica and I are into skater stuff.

Trend Are you wearing those shorts because it's hot, or because they're trendy?!

Johnny Because I really like the colour!

Trend I see. Cool. Billy, you aren't wearing trendy clothes today! Is that your school uniform?

Billy Yes, our uniform at Green Park School is this blue jumper, white shirt, grey trousers and tie.

Trend Do you like wearing school uniform?

Billy It's not very cool, but it's only for school. I don't mind it. In the evening I always wear a tracksuit and trainers! I'm not very interested in clothes.

Trend And you, Beatrice?

Beatrice Well, I hate the skirt and white socks – I look like a kid! – but the uniform is practical. I love clothes – especially shoes! – but I keep my designer stuff for weekends. I'm shopping for a new dress and sandals now – for an eighteenth birthday party.

Trend Enjoy your shopping then!

Beatrice Thanks!

1 Look at the photos. Who's wearing…
   a a vest top?   b a T-shirt?   c a uniform?

2 🔊 1.54 Read and listen to the interview with *Trend* magazine. Which two teenagers are students at Green Park School?

FLASH FORWARD
What clothes do you like wearing at school/at weekends?

3 Read the interview again and write in the table what the people are wearing.

Name	Clothes
Jessica	
Johnny	
Billy	
Beatrice	

50

4

GRAMMAR

Present continuous

He's **wearing** shorts.
You **aren't wearing** trendy clothes.
Are you **wearing** these for school?

Find more examples of the Present continuous in the text. Underline them.

4 Complete the sentences with the Present continuous of the verbs below.

have	play	not listen
go	learn	not wear

1 I *am going* to school.
2 We _____ jeans.
3 You _____ to the teacher.
4 Listen! He _____ the piano.
5 _____ she _____ English?
6 I _____ coffee with friends.

Vocabulary: Clothes and accessories

5 🔊 1.55 Look at the pictures and complete the words. Then listen and check.

1 sh__ __t
2 jack__ __
3 t__o__sers
4 sh__ __s
5 ski__ __
6 d__ __ss
7 c__a__
8 jump__ __
9 tr__ __ner__

6 🔊 1.56 Look at the pictures and complete the descriptions of the people with the words below, then listen and check your answers.

| tie | belt | sunglasses | boots | scarf | hat | gloves |

Laura Valerie Richard

1 Laura is wearing leggings, a T-shirt, trainers, and black _____ .
2 Valerie is wearing a dress with a _____ , a green _____ and cowboy _____ .
3 Richard is wearing a coat, a shirt with a red and blue _____ , brown _____ and a black _____ .

7 What do clothes say about personality? Match the descriptions with the correct pictures in exercise 6.

a ☐ This person likes flirting, loves going to discos and having a good time.
b ☐ This person enjoys making money, is a successful manager and is serious.
c ☐ This person likes running and playing sports.

Say it!

8 Choose a person in your class and describe what he/she is wearing today. Talk about clothes and accessories. Can your classmates guess who it is?

A *This person is wearing jeans and a white T-shirt with a blue jumper.*
B *Is he wearing black trainers too?*
A *Yes, he is.*
B *Philip?*
A *Yes!*

51

4

I'm looking for a miniskirt

1 🔊 1.57 Listen and read the two dialogues. Where is Anna in each situation? What is she doing?

Assistant	Can I help you?
Anna	Yes, please. Can I try this top on?
Assistant	Sure. Anything else?
Anna	I'm looking for a miniskirt too.
Assistant	Yes, certainly, what size are you looking for?
Anna	Size 10.
Assistant	What about this style? It's casual and we've got it in floral cotton too.
Anna	Oh, yes, what a lovely style! Have you got it in other colours?

Later, at home

Anna	Hi, Dad. I'm going out now.
Dad	Are you going out again?
Anna	Yes Dad, I always go out on Friday. It's my night off.
Dad	Are you wearing that skirt?
Anna	Yes, I am. It's new – I've got a date…
Dad	A date?
Anna	Bye. See you at twelve.
Dad	At twelve midnight?
Anna	Dad, I'm 16! Anyway, Antonio's waiting for me. Bye!

2 Correct these statements.

1 The shop assistant is trying on clothes.
   The shop assistant isn't trying on clothes, Anna is trying on clothes.
2 Anna is looking for a red dress.
3 Anna works on Friday night.
4 Anna's dad is getting dressed to go out.
5 Tonight, Anna is watching TV at home.

3 Answer the questions.

1 What two things does Anna want to buy?
2 What size is she?
3 What is she wearing for her date?
4 What does her dad think about it?
5 Who is she going out with?

FLASH FORWARD

Write the answers in ex. 3 in your notebook.

Vocabulary: Adjectives for clothes

4 ◉ 1.58 Write the adjectives under the pictures, then listen, check your answers and repeat.

| striped | patterned | floral | cotton | checked | plain |
| tight | leather | loose | woollen | casual | smart |

1 _____ 2  _____ 3 _____
4  _____ 5  _____ 6 _____ 
7  _____ 8  _____ 9 _____ 
10  _____ 11  _____ 12 _____ 

FUNCTIONS

Shopping for clothes

Can I help you?
Anything else?
What size are you looking for?
What about this style?

Can I try this top on?
I'm looking for a miniskirt too.
Have you got it in other colours too?

Say it!

5 Work in pairs. Make dialogues using the expressions from the box and different words for clothes, sizes and colours.

GRAMMAR

Present continuous vs Present simple

I'm going out **now**.
They're living in Dublin **at the moment**.

I **always** go out on Friday.
He **often** visits us in the summer.

Find more examples of the Present continuous and underline them, then find examples of the Present simple and circle them.

6 Choose the correct tense, Present continuous or Present simple.

1 I *go/am going* to school by bus.
2 I *get up/am getting up* at 7 o'clock and I get dressed.
3 Look at that strange man! He *wears/is wearing* punk clothes.
4 Where is Anna now? She *talks/is talking* on the phone.
5 I *often go/am often going* on holiday with my parents.
6 I *don't speak/am not speaking* good English.
7 They're *working/work* late this week.

Say it!

7 Work in pairs. Ask about the people in your friend's family. What are they doing now? What are they wearing? What do they usually do at weekends? What do they wear?

A *What's your mum doing now?*
B *I think my mum's working in the office.*
A *What's she wearing?*
B *She's wearing a purple jumper and a smart striped shirt.*
A *What does your mum usually do at the weekends?*
B *At the weekends, she usually does work in the house.*
A *What does she wear?*
B *She wears casual clothes: a green tracksuit...*

4 Vocabulary Workshop

Clothes and accessories

1 Write the words in the correct column.

> tie   belt   sunglasses   boots   scarf   hat
> gloves   sandals   shirt   jacket   trousers
> shoes   skirt   dress   coat   jumper

Clothes	Accessories
boots (P)	

2 Which of the words in exercise 1 are singular and which are plural? Write S or P next to the word.

3 Look at the picture of Jennifer's wardrobe for one minute. What clothes and accessories can you remember?

A brown coat, a green skirt…

STUDY SKILLS
Using a dictionary (1)

When you look up a new word in a dictionary there is often more than one meaning. To identify which meaning is correct, first look at the context of the word. Check the grammar: is it a noun, a verb, an adjective or an adverb?

Is there an article before it? e.g. *a/an/the* → noun
Is there an auxiliary verb before it?
e.g. *am/is/doesn't/don't* → verb
Does it describe a person or thing? → adjective
Does it describe an action? → adverb

4 Read the text. Are the words in blue nouns, verbs, adjectives or adverbs?

'I spend most of the money on designer clothes – I love them! I go to outlets where designer clothes are cheap. I usually find a lot of good stuff because I'm a size 10. I don't wear designer gear to school, I only wear it when I go out with my friends clubbing or at parties. I like clothes but I love shoes! I've got fifty pairs of shoes and trainers, some of them are vintage. When I'm at home I love chilling out on the sofa in an old tracksuit and a pair of my favourite trainers!'

1 outlet: _noun_   4 gear: _____
2 cheap: _____   5 clubbing: _____
3 usually: _____   6 chilling out: _____

Pronunciation: /tʃ/ and /ʃ/

5 🔊 1.59 Listen and repeat the words.

/tʃ/	/ʃ/
cheap, choose, chilling, much, catch, _____	shirt, shoes, shilling, hush, cash, _____

6 🔊 1.60 Now listen and add these words to the chart in exercise 5.

> sheep   church   check   shower   sure
> touch   show   furniture   children   push

7 🔊 1.61 Now listen, check your answers and repeat the words.

Spoken English

To express surprise, admiration or disgust we use:

What a/an + (adjective) + singular noun.
What + (adjective) + plural noun or uncountable noun.

What a cool look!
What beautiful shoes!

8 Look at the pictures and make exclamations with *What* + an adjective.

1 _____   2 _____   3 _____

54

Flash on Grammar 4

Present continuous

Affirmative

I	'm	
He/She/It	's	going.
You/We/They	're	

Negative

I	'm not	
He/She/It	isn't	going.
You/We/They	aren't	

Interrogative

Am	I	
Is	he/she/it	going?
Are	we/you/they	

Short answers

Yes, I am./No, I'm not.

Wh- questions

Who are you talking to?   **Why** are you crying?
Where are you going?   **How** are you driving?
What are you eating?

We use the Present continuous to describe an action taking place at the moment of speaking or to describe temporary situations.
I **am reading** a book now.
She**'s studying** for her exams these days.

WB p. 32

1 Complete the sentences with the Present continuous of the verbs below. Be careful, there are two more.

> ~~go~~   play   write   look for
> wear   wash   ring   learn

1 He *'s going* to school.
2 She _____ her hair.
3 He _____ an email.
4 We _____ English and French.
5 They _____ a new house.
6 Her mobile phone _____ .

2 Write the sentences in ex. 1 in the negative form.

3 Complete the sentences with the Present continuous form of the verbs in brackets.

1 Sam *isn't sleeping* (sleep), he _____ (watch) TV.
2 The boys _____ (do) their homework, they _____ (play) games on the computer.
3 Lisa _____ (write) in her notebook, she _____ (read) a magazine.
4 My parents _____ (cook) dinner, they _____ (walk) in the park.
5 Rachel _____ (play) the piano, she _____ (listen) to a CD.
6 I _____ (have) a bath, I _____ (have) a shower.

Present simple vs Present continuous

- We use the Present simple to talk about a habit or daily routine. It is often used with adverbs of frequency like *always*, *usually*, etc. and time expressions like *every day/week*, *once a day/week*, etc.

- We use the Present continuous to talk about actions taking place at the time of speaking and it is often used with time expressions like *now*, *at the moment*, *today*, *tonight*, *this week*, etc.

I usually **read** a book before I go to bed, but tonight I**'m watching** TV.

WB p. 33

4 Complete the email with the Present simple or the Present continuous of the verbs in brackets.

Hi Kath,
How are you? What (1) *are you doing* (you/do)? The weather in London is awful today.
It (2) _____ (rain) again. It (3) _____ (rain) every day here! Right now, I (4) _____ (not work) in the B'n'B. I (5) _____ (work) from Monday to Thursday but today is Saturday, my day off! I usually (6) _____ out with my friends on Saturday night but tonight I (7) _____ (not go out), I (8) _____ (stay) at home to watch a DVD with Antonio. Not very romantic but we (9) _____ (not have) any money this week!
Write soon!
Love,
Anna

5 Make questions about Anna's email using the prompts.

1 Anna / have breakfast?
   Is Anna having breakfast?
2 what / she / do?
3 it / rain / today / in London?
4 Anna / work / in the B&B / Saturdays?
5 what / Anna and Antonio / do / tonight?

6 Now answer the questions in exercise 5.

7 Write sentences which are true for you with the words below. Use time expressions.

1 sun / shine
   The sun is shining now.
2 it / rain
3 I / wear / jeans
4 I / speak / English
5 my friend / talk
6 my mobile / ring

55

4 Flash on Skills

Retail therapy

Before you read

1 Complete the sentences about your city or country.

1 A famous supermarket is _____ .
2 A famous clothes shop is _____ .
3 A cheap market is _____ .
4 A second hand shop is _____ .

Reading

2 Read the information about shopping in Britain. Match the paragraphs to the photos.

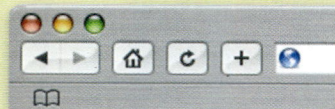

A Visitor's Guide to Shopping in Britain

1 ☐ Department stores

The Brits love these exclusive stores – they are really just enormous shops on many floors – everything is under one roof! *Harrod's* in London is the most famous department store in the country: it sells everything from expensive designer clothes to pets, furniture and ice cream! Other stores like *Harvey Nicol's*, *House of Fraser* and *John Lewis* have got branches in the major cities and often have cafés and restaurants in them too.

2 ☐ High Street chains

Most people you see in the streets of Britain are probably wearing underwear from Marks and Spencer's and buy all their food from Tesco's! These big companies have got shops on the main streets of all large towns and cities, so a lot of British people shop there. The goods are the same in each shop but prices are reasonable, and they offer extra services to customers like free home delivery.

3 ☐ Outdoor markets in London

In a lot of cities there are still traditional markets. These are usually one or two times a week and sell everything from apples to antiques! They are cheap and colourful and a good place to meet local people and try traditional British food. Some markets specialise in certain types of goods. For example, Berwick Street Market near Piccadilly Circus sells fruit, vegetables, sweets and cheeses, while Brick Lane Market has a mix of old furniture, books and music.

4 ☐ Charity shops

The British are very enthusiastic about recycling and there are a lot of charity shops in every town – people donate old clothes and goods (books, CDs, bric-a-brac) and the shops then sell them. The money they make goes to the charity – Oxfam, Save the Children, Cancer Relief, etc. The prices are very cheap and you're sure to find surprising bargains in these places, from a vintage Dior dress, to an original Elvis Presley record.

Culture 4

3 Read the statements and write T (true) or F (false), then correct the false statements.

1 Department stores sell a variety of things. ___
2 All the departments are on one floor. ___
3 Chain stores have only got shops in London. ___
4 They are very expensive. ___
5 Only tourists shop in outdoor markets. ___
6 Many of them also sell food. ___
7 People give things they don't want to charity shops. ___
8 The money from charity shops goes to help other people. ___

Listening

4 🔊 1.62 Listen to a woman talking about an unusual type of shop she works in. Where is it?

1 London Zoo   3 The British Museum
2 Buckingham Palace

5 🔊 1.62 Listen again. Which of these things do they sell in the shop? (✓)

| bags | sweets | pens | tea | notebooks | jewellery | coins |
| vases | clothes | CDs | statues | books | toys | puzzles |

6 Answer the questions.

1 What type of people shop in this shop?
2 What's unusual about the jewellery they sell there?
3 What sort of books have they got?

STUDY SKILLS
Taking notes

Taking notes is an extremely useful skill if you learn to do it well. Read the text once then read the exercise/exam question. Plan your notes before you begin. Think about why you are taking the notes. What are they for? Think about types of information which could be useful to help you in the task. Write these down in the form of headings or questions. Now read the text again and find information related to these headings/questions.

Task: Read the text and write about different kinds of shops in England.

Headings: Department stores, High Street chain, Outdoor markets, Charity shops.

Writing

7 Use your answers to exercise 1 to write information for tourists about shopping in your town. Use the text in exercise 2 as a model. Make notes to help you under these headings.

- What type of shops are there?
- Where are they?
- What goods do they sell?
- Are they cheap or expensive?
- Do they sell traditional or modern goods?

In the USA, New York is the capital of shopping...

Speaking

8 Use your writing from exercise 7 to report back to the class about shopping in your area.

57

Flashback

GRAMMAR
Adverbs of frequency

1 Look at the diagram and complete the sentences with the best adverb.

0%		50%			100%
never	hardly ever	sometimes	often	usually	always

0 I _never_ (0%) eat meat. I'm a vegetarian.
1 I _____ (99%) go to school by bus.
2 I _____ (100%) go to bed at night.
3 I _____ (2%) take a taxi to school.
4 I _____ (99%) have breakfast.
5 I _____ (80%) have a big breakfast.
6 I _____ (50%) go to the cinema at weekends.

☐ 6

2 Look at the chart and complete the sentences with an appropriate adverb.

> every weekend   every day (x2)   ~~twice a week~~
> three times a week   once a week   never
> every Sunday   four times a week

My ideal holiday...

Sunday	swimming ice cream play sports go sightseeing get up late go on picnic
Monday	swimming ice cream visit monuments get up late
Tuesday	swimming play sports get up late
Wednesday	swimming get up late
Thursday	swimming get up late
Friday	swimming ice cream visit monuments cinema get up late
Saturday	swimming ice cream play sports go sightseeing get up late

0 She visits monuments _twice a week_ .
1 She goes sightseeing _____ .
2 She plays sports _____ .
3 She goes swimming _____ .
4 She gets up late _____ .
5 She eats ice cream _____ .
6 She goes on picnics _____ .
7 She goes to the cinema _____ .
8 She _____ does homework.

☐ 8

Verbs of preference + -ing

3 Complete the sentences. Use the correct form of the verbs below.

> ~~listen~~ speak get up travel do go play

0 I like _listening_ to music.
1 I don't like _____ to the dentist.
2 I love _____ computer games.
3 I don't enjoy _____ early.
4 I don't mind _____ English.
5 I hate _____ homework.
6 I can't stand _____ by air.

☐ 6

Object pronouns

4 Read the sentences, then complete the second version with the correct object pronoun.

0 I love listening to my MP3 player. I love listening to _it_ .
1 I don't like tests. I don't like _____ .
2 I like my bedroom. I like _____ .
3 I love my best friend, Helena. I love _____ .
4 I enjoy watching football. I enjoy watching _____ .
5 I see Paul every day. I see _____ every day.
6 Ms Smith teaches our class English. She teaches _____ English.

☐ 6

Present continuous

5 Complete the sentences with the present continuous of the verbs below.

> ~~go~~ (x2) play write look for wear
> wash ring learn buy speak

0 They'_re going_ to school now.
1 They _____ their keys; where are they?
2 Italy _____ against Spain in the Eurocup now.
3 It's her birthday today and she _____ her best clothes.
4 Silvia _____ a letter to her grandmother in America.
5 Maria and I _____ our hair – we have a date!
6 I'm at the shops and I _____ a new laptop.
7 The telephone _____ – answer it!
8 At school we _____ English, Maths and History.
9 Hi, Maria! I _____ to the doctor – I don't feel well.
10 Mum, I'm busy now! I _____ to Antonio on the phone.

☐ 10

Flashback 3 4

Present simple vs Present continuous

6 Underline the correct option.

0 'Where *do you go/are you going*?' 'To the market.'
1 Every day I *'m talking/talk* to John on the phone.
2 What *do you read/are you reading* now?
3 Why *do you study/are you studying* so hard these days?
4 We *go/'re going* to the cinema every weekend.
5 My mum *doesn't work/isn't working* at the moment, she's on holiday.

[5]

Round up!

7 Complete the dialogue using the words below.

| once | do | who | stand | see | are |
| always | ~~doing~~ | walking | riding | come |

Eva   Hi, how are you?
Tony I'm fine. What are you (0) *doing* here?
Eva   Oh, I (1) _____ come here on Saturdays.
Tony Yes, I come every day too. It's great. I like (2) _____ in the park.
Eva   I usually (3) _____ on my bike. I love (4) _____ my bike here.
Tony How (5) _____ you doing at your new school?
Eva   I'm enjoying it but I can't (6) _____ the maths teacher.
Tony (7) _____ are you going out with now?
Eva   Oh, I see John (8) _____ or twice a week but…
Tony … you're just good friends.
Eva   Right. Are you still going out with Pauline?
Tony Yeah, I (9) _____ her three or four times a week.
Eva   Where are you going now?
Tony I'm free. (10) _____ you want to go for coffee?

[10]

VOCABULARY
Holiday accommodation and transport

8 Complete the sentences with the words below.

| ~~hotel~~ | bed and breakfast | tent | bus | taxi | ferry |

0 We usually stay in an expensive *hotel* when I'm on holiday with my parents.
1 When we go to Greece, we usually go by ship or by _____ .
2 In London, we stay in a youth hostel or a _____ because it's not expensive.
3 When we go camping, we stay in a _____ .
4 When she's late for work, she takes a _____ but it's very expensive.
5 I usually walk to school, but when it is raining I take the _____ .

[5]

Clothes

9 Complete the names of clothes and accessories.

0 gl o v e s
1 sh _ _ s
2 tro _ _ _ _ _
3 sh _ _ _
4 be _ _
5 s _ _ _ t
6 dr _ _ _ _
7 c _ _ t
8 sc _ _ _ _
9 j _ _ _ _ _ r
10 tra _ _ _ _ _ s
11 b _ _ _ s
12 ja _ _ _ _ _
13 h _ _
14 su _ _ _ _ _ _ _ _ s
15 t _ _ .

[15]

10 Find the adjectives for clothes.

0 mtasr   *smart*   6 stidpre   _____
1 atrnetedp _____   7 cdhckee   _____
2 gtith   _____   8 cttoon   _____
3 rfolal   _____   9 lewloon   _____
4 csalua   _____   10 leharte _____
5 pnlia   _____   11 lsooe   _____

[11]

FUNCTIONS
Asking for travel information

11 Complete these dialogues.

A Excuse (0) *me* , does this bus (1) _____ to Trafalgar Square?
B No, it doesn't. You (2) _____ bus 23. It's three (3) _____ from here.
A Does the 22 (4) _____ there, too?
B No, the 22 (5) _____ to Covent Garden.
A (6) _____ do you get to the National museum from here?
B Take the tube; you want the Piccadilly (7) _____ . It's three (8) _____ from here.

[8]

Shopping for clothes

12 Unscramble the dialogue.

[1] Can I help you?
[ ] Yes, it's nice. Have you got it in different colours?
[ ] Yes, of course.
[ ] It's a bit small. Have you got it in a different size?
[ ] What style are you looking for?
[ ] I'm looking for a checked shirt.
[ ] Yes, I am looking for a shirt.
[ ] What about this black and red shirt?
[ ] Can I try it on?
[ ] Sorry, that's the last one.
[ ] Yes, we've got this blue and white one, too.

[10]

Total: [100]

5 You Are What You Eat...

British food sucks! Fact or fiction?

1 Match the photos below to the words.

1. ☐ sushi
2. ☐ fish and chips
3. ☐ chicken tikka masala
4. ☐ roast beef and Yorkshire pudding

2 We all know horror stories about the British and their food but society is changing and the diet is too. How much do you know about British cuisine? What is fact and what is fiction? Do our quiz!

1. Fish and chips is the national dish. **Yes No**
2. The British don't like food from other countries. **Yes No**
3. The restaurants in Britain are very expensive. **Yes No**
4. There aren't any typical British dishes. **Yes No**
5. The British eat enormous breakfasts. **Yes No**
6. Tea is the number one drink in the UK. **Yes No**

3 🔘 2.02 Now read and listen to the text and check your answers to the quiz.

1 The favourite dish in the UK is now chicken tikka masala, a curry dish of roast chicken in a red, spicy, tomato sauce.

2 It isn't true that there isn't much variety in the British diet, the British love eating foreign food and especially popular are Italian, Chinese and Thai food. There are also a lot of ready-made foreign dishes in supermarkets and restaurants and the new fast food in Britain today is sushi!

3 There are some very expensive restaurants but fish and chips costs just a few pounds! There are also Indian and Chinese restaurants – they serve cheap, tasty food.

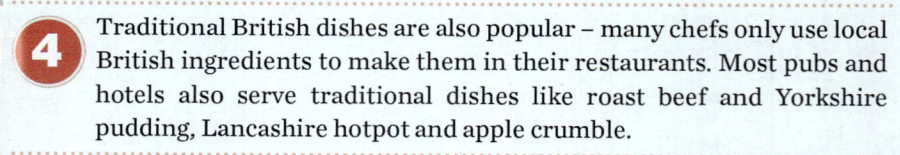

4 Traditional British dishes are also popular – many chefs only use local British ingredients to make them in their restaurants. Most pubs and hotels also serve traditional dishes like roast beef and Yorkshire pudding, Lancashire hotpot and apple crumble.

5 At home, most people usually have a light breakfast – coffee or tea and toast or cereal – but some people eat more at weekends. Hotels and cafés serve the traditional 'Full English Breakfast' of bacon, sausage, eggs, tomatoes and mushrooms but it's for the tourists!

6 Tea is originally from India but of course it's the favourite drink in Britain. The British love tea – with milk and a little sugar! Some people drink 6 or 7 cups a day!

4 Answer these questions.

1. What are the ingredients of England's favourite dish?
2. What are the three most popular types of foreign food in the UK?
3. Which type of food is not expensive in UK restaurants?
4. Write the names of three traditional British dishes.
5. What do British people usually have for breakfast?

FLASH FORWARD

What are the ingredients of a favourite dish from your country? Write a list.

Vocabulary: Food and drink

5 🔊 **2.03** Listen and repeat the words. Which of these ingredients are there in the English Breakfast in the photo? (✓)

- ☐ sausages
- ☐ bacon
- ☐ eggs
- ☐ beans
- ☐ milk
- ☐ cheese
- ☐ toast
- ☐ cereal
- ☐ mushrooms
- ☐ tea
- ☐ coffee
- ☐ yoghurt
- ☐ pasta
- ☐ fruit juice
- ☐ pastries
- ☐ cake
- ☐ tomatoes
- ☐ biscuits

6 Look at the other words in exercise 5. Can you guess their meanings? Compare with your partner.

FLASHPOINT

Countable nouns indicate things that can be counted and they have both a singular and a plural form:
an apple   three apples

Uncountable nouns indicate things that cannot be counted in numbers and they are used in the singular form:
sugar, salt, water, milk, air, happiness

7 Which words in ex. 5 are countable and which are uncountable? Write the words in the correct column.

Countable	Uncountable
sausages, _____	bacon, _____
_____	_____
_____	_____
_____	_____

GRAMMAR

some/any

There are **some** very expensive restaurants.
There aren't **any** typical British dishes.
Are there **any** tomatoes in the fridge?

Find examples of *some* and *any* in the text. Underline them.

8 Complete the sentences with *some* or *any*.
1. Is there _____ milk in the bottle?
2. Yes, there are _____ bars in this street.
3. Is there _____ food in the kitchen?
4. There is _____ strange sauce on the chicken.
5. Have we got _____ eggs for the crepes?
6. Are there _____ sushi bars in Brent Street?
7. We haven't got _____ cheese for the pizza!
8. There aren't _____ good restaurants in our town.

Say it!

9 Talk about your favourite breakfast. What do you like to eat in the morning? What do you usually have?

I usually have some cereal for breakfast and I love yoghurt! I don't like any hot drinks, I always drink milk...

Write it!

10 Write about the differences between the typical breakfast in your country and the Full English Breakfast. What do they serve for breakfast in hotels and bars?

In France they serve cappuccinos, croissants...

5

How many eggs are there?

1 🔘 **2.04** Read and listen to the dialogue.
What are Antonio and Anna writing?

Anna	Yuk! There's too much sugar in this coffee!
Antonio	And there isn't any sugar in my coffee! Yuk!
Anna	I think this is your coffee, Antonio! Swap?
Antonio	Okay. Mmm... that's better. Now, the shopping. Have we got any cereal?
Anna	Well, there isn't much...
Antonio	Okay. Three packets of cereal. Now, are there any eggs?
Anna	Well, there are a few... but there aren't enough for breakfast.
Antonio	How many eggs are there?
Anna	Not many – four.
Antonio	Let's get three dozen.
Anna	No, three dozen are too many, Antonio! Two dozen are enough.
Antonio	Okay, you're the boss. Are there any sausages?
Anna	Yes, there are enough sausages, I think, but there isn't much cheese.
Antonio	Right, a kilo of cheese...
Anna	No, that's too much cheese! Write half a kilo.
Antonio	Half a kilo of cheese. And how much sugar is there?
Anna	Sugar? There's a lot of sugar – look! Four packets!
Antonio	'Ah, sugar, sugar, you are my candy girl...'
Anna	Antonio, stop it! Dad's coming.
Henry	What's going on here?
Antonio	Nothing. Antonio's helping me, Dad.

2 What things does Anna need for the B&B? Put a tick (✓) or a cross (✗).

Shopping list
1 bacon
2 eggs
3 sausages
4 cheese
5 beans
6 sugar
7 milk
8 cereal
9 coffee

FLASH FORWARD

What are the typical ingredients you use in cooking? Write a list.

I use a lot of cheese, tomatoes, olive oil...

GRAMMAR

How much/many...? – too much/many

How many eggs are there?
How much sugar is there?

There's **too much** sugar in this coffee.
Three dozen are **too many**.

Find examples of *How much/many?* and *too much/many* in the dialogue and underline them.

3 Underline the correct word in each sentence.

1 How *many/much* biscuits are there in the cupboard?
2 How *much/many* tea is there in the teapot?
3 How *much/many* litres of water are there in that bottle?
4 There are too *much/many* people in here.
5 There are too *much/many* apples in the basket.

GRAMMAR

a lot of, a little, a few, not much/many, enough

Countables
Are there any eggs?
There are **a lot of** eggs.
There are **enough** eggs.
There are **a few** eggs.
There are**n't many** eggs.
There are**n't enough** eggs.

Uncountables
Is there any bacon?
There's **a lot of** bacon.
There's **enough** bacon.
There's **a little** bacon.
There is**n't much** bacon.
There is**n't enough** bacon.

Find examples of *a lot of, a little, a few, not much/many* and *enough* in the dialogue. Circle them.

FUNCTIONS

Talking about quantities

How much sugar is there?
There's a lot of sugar.

4 Make questions about this picture with *how much/many*, then answer them with *a little/a few*, *not much/many*, *a lot of*, *enough*.

A *How many eggs are there?*
B *There are enough.*

A *How much tea is there?*
B *There's a lot.*

Vocabulary: Containers and packages

5 🔊 2.05 Complete with the words in the box. Then listen and check.

slice loaf bag tin packet
jar bottle carton can

1 a *jar* of jam
2 a _____ of water 
3 a _____ of bread 
4 a _____ of apples 
5 a _____ of fruit juice 
6 a _____ of cola 
7 a _____ of beans 
8 a _____ of biscuits 
9 a _____ of pie 

Say it!

6 Look at the food pyramid. Do you have a healthy or unhealthy diet? In pairs, ask and answer.

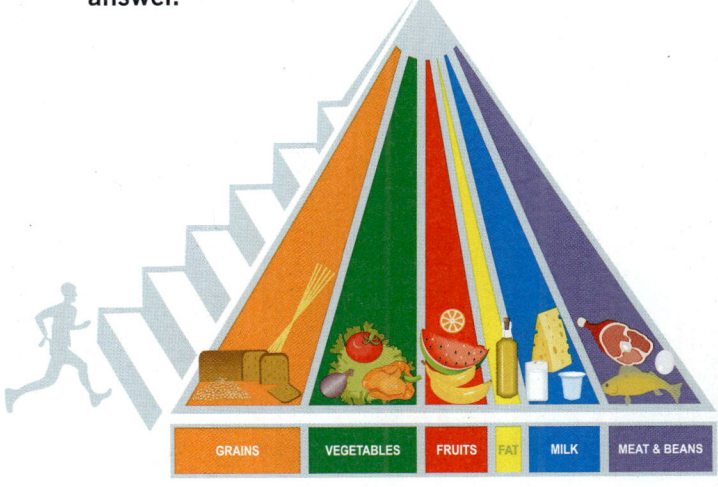

GRAINS   VEGETABLES   FRUITS   FAT   MILK   MEAT & BEANS

A *Do you have a healthy diet?*
B *Yes, I eat a lot of fruit, but I also love biscuits!*
A *How many packets of biscuits do you eat in a week?*
B *About four packets.*

5 Vocabulary Workshop

Food and drink

1 Look again at the food pyramid on page 63 and complete the table with all the words you know.

Grains	Vegetables	Fruits
cereal, _____ _____	tomatoes, _____	apples, _____

Fats	Milk products	Meats & Beans
oil, _____ _____	cheese, _____	chicken, _____

2 Match the units of measurement with their abbreviations.

1 grammes   a 2 kg
2 pounds   b 500 gms
3 kilograms   c 3 lbs
4 litres   d 400 ml
5 millilitres   e 5 l

3 What type of food do we use the units of measurement in exercise 3 for? Write a list.

grammes: sugar, flour

4 🔘 **2.06** Mrs Granger shops online on the Fresco's supermarket website. Listen to her conversation with the Fresco's manager and complete the dialogue.

Mrs Granger Good morning, is that Fresco's supermarket?
Manager Yes, madam, it is. How can I help you?
Mrs Granger It's my online shopping order. This week a lot of things are missing…
Manager I'm very sorry, madam. Which items are missing?
Mrs Granger Well, there's too much (1) _____ – four packets but I only need two – and there isn't any cheese. And there isn't much milk – just one carton but I need three. Then there aren't any biscuits or yoghurt but there's a lot of (2) _____ .
Manager How much bacon is there?
Mrs Granger Three packets.
Manager And how many packets of biscuits do you want?
Mrs Granger Two packets.
Manager Right. Anything else?
Mrs Granger Yes, I need a tin of coffee – 450 grams – and a loaf of bread but I don't want the (3) _____ . There are a dozen (4) _____ ! Then there's too much…

5 Complete the order with the things Mrs Granger wants.

Fresco's Online Delivery Service — *Fresh to your door!*

Name: _____
Email Address: _____
Date: 18/11/2011
Order: _____

Items

2 packets of _____
500 gms of cheese
3 cartons of _____
2 packets of _____
1 carton of yoghurt
450 gms of coffee
1 loaf of _____

6 Write an online food order then dictate it to your partner. Compare your lists. Are they the same? Are the quantities correct?

Five packets of biscuits. Three bottles of water…

Pronunciation: word stress

Generally, in words with two syllables, the stress falls on the first syllable in nouns and on the second syllable in verbs.

7 🔘 **2.07** Listen and repeat the words.

● •	• ●
problem, water, _____	receive, record, _____

8 🔘 **2.08** Listen and write the words in the correct column in exercise 7.

bacon   coffee   biscuit   believe   complete
shopping   enjoy   packet   compare   create
prefer   carton   apple   bottle

9 🔘 **2.09** Now listen, check your answers and repeat the words.

Flash on Grammar 5

some/any

	Countable	Uncountable
Affirmative	There are **some** eggs.	We've got **some** cheese.
Negative	There aren't **any** beans.	We haven't got **any** bacon.
Questions	Are there **any** beans? Would you like **some** tea?	Have we got **any** bacon? Can you give me **some** money?

WB p. 40

1 Complete the sentences with *a/an*, *some*, *any*.

1 She is reading *a* book.
2 She is buying _____ books.
3 I haven't got _____ money.
4 Are there _____ chips on the menu?
5 There isn't _____ tea in the cup.
6 We have got _____ spaghetti.

2 Look at the cupboard and make sentences with *a/an*, *some*, *any* and the words in the box.

apple
bread
bananas
tomatoes
sugar
cheese
pasta
potatoes
cereal
biscuits

There is an apple in the cupboard.

How much/many + quantities

	Uncountable	Countable
Questions	**How much** sugar is there?	**How many** eggs are there?
Large quantities	There's **too much** sugar. There's **a lot of/ enough** sugar.	There are **too many** eggs. There are **a lot of/ enough** eggs.
Small quantities	There isn't **much**/ **not enough** sugar. There's **a little** sugar.	There aren't **many**/ **not enough** eggs. There are **a few** eggs.

WB p. 40

3 Complete the sentences with *how much/many*, then answer the questions.

1 _____ girls are there in your class?
2 _____ students are not from your town originally?
3 _____ people in your family wear glasses?
4 _____ is a kilogram of cheese?
5 _____ books have you got in your schoolbag today?
6 _____ homework have you got to do tonight?

4 Complete the mini-dialogues with *much/many/ a lot of/a little/a few/enough*.

Fran   How (1) *many* friends do you have on Facebook, Beryl?
Beryl   About a million. In fact I have too (2) _____ – I don't have (3) _____ time for them!
Fran   And how (4) _____ real friends do you have?
Beryl   Real friends? Actually, I've got (5) _____ real friends, not many, 3 or 4.

Dan   Do you eat a lot, Paul?
Paul   Yeah, I eat too (6) _____ ! I have a big breakfast but I only eat (7) _____ food at lunchtime.
Dan   What's your favourite dish?
Paul   Oh, I don't like (8) _____ dishes. Just pasta, pasta and pasta!
Dan   Do you eat (9) _____ cheese?
Paul   Actually, I only eat (10) _____ cheese and I don't eat (11) _____ yoghurt or milk.

5 Complete the summary of the text on page 60 with expressions of quantity.

In English cuisine, there's (1) _____ variety. (2) _____ British people like foreign food. There are (3) _____ fast food restaurants in the UK but there are also (4) _____ Italian, Indian and Chinese restaurants.
Nowadays at home British people don't eat (5) _____ for breakfast. They usually have coffee or tea and toast or cereal. But in (6) _____ hotels they still serve the 'Full English Breakfast' – and that is (7) _____ of food!! Tea is still the favourite drink in England. The British love tea and they drink (8) _____ cups of tea – about 6 every day!

6 🔊 2.10 **Listen and check your answers.**

65

5 Flash on Skills

GM Foods – What are the dangers?

Before you read

1 Match the food words with the correct photos.

1 ☐ wheat   3 ☐ chicken   5 ☐ rice
2 ☐ beef   4 ☐ grapes

Reading

2 Read the text and tick (✓) the correct definition of GM food.

a ☐ New types of plants and animals with no DNA.
b ☐ New types of plants with animal DNA in them.
c ☐ New types of plants or animals which scientists create with changes to their DNA.

In some countries, like the USA, people already eat a lot of GM food. At breakfast, the milk on their cornflakes probably comes from a genetically modified cow, and the cereal in those corn flakes probably comes from genetically modified corn. At lunch, many Americans eat genetically modified beef, chicken or ham on their sandwiches, or in their salads, every day and drink fruit juice made from genetically modified fruit. Perhaps the wine they drink with their dinner comes from genetically modified grapes, and the rice or pasta they eat is from GM crops too. Is this a good thing, or a bad thing?

How many people understand exactly what GM technology means? At the moment, there is a lot of controversy about GM foods. Basically, in all types of GM technology scientists take a gene from a plant or animal and they put it into a different plant or animal. In this way, they create new organisms. This process produces new varieties of organisms – these can resist diseases – farmers grow more crops with GM technology, and these crops stay fresh for a long time.

GM technology is good for the environment, too. The crops don't need a lot of pesticides, fertilizers and water to grow. In poor countries, where millions of people are dying of hunger, a small amount of land can produce a large amount of very nutritious food.

So, why is there all this alarm about GM technology? What other consequences does human interference with Nature create?

CLIL 5

STUDY SKILLS
Reading for gist (2)

In understanding the gist of a text it can help to find the topic sentence in each paragraph or section. The topic sentences usually use language related to that of the title, and express the different aspects, or points in the argument, which the writer is exploring in each different part of his text.

3 Read the text again and underline the topic sentence in each of the two main paragraphs.

4 Read the statements and write T (true) or F (false), then correct the false statements.
1. Americans don't eat any GM food.
2. GM technology mixes genes from different organisms. This creates new organisms.
3. GM crops produce more food than non-GM crops.
4. GM technology helps to protect animals and plants from diseases.
5. GM crops grow where there is only a little water.
6. GM food is not very nutritious.

5 Answer the questions.
1. How do scientists create genetically modified organisms?
2. Why do GM crops produce more food?
3. Why is GM technology good for the environment?
4. How can the technology help people in poor countries?

Listening

6 🔊 2.11 Listen to part of a radio interview with an American doctor about her opinions on GM foods. Does she think GM foods are good or bad?

7 🔊 2.11 Listen again and complete the summary with the words below.

| effects | humans | cause | diversity | insects |
| know | crops | resistant | ecosystem | animals |

Scientists know that GM crops often contaminate other (1) _____ . They dominate the (2) _____ because they are strong and (3) _____ to diseases. Other plants die and then there is no (4) _____ in the plant life of a particular area and (5) _____ and (6) _____ die because they can't find appropriate plants to eat. GM crops also sometimes (7) _____ allergies because they produce new types of pollen; (8) _____ are sensitive to this new pollen. However the main worry about GM technology is its (9) _____ on humans in the future. We don't (10) _____ if GM food is really safe.

Writing

8 Look at the text about GM food again and the summary from the radio interview. Underline the pros and cons of the technology. Write a list in the two columns.

For GM technology	Against GM technology
_____	_____
_____	_____
_____	_____

Speaking

9 What do you think about GM technology? Are you for it or against it? Do a class survey and form two groups, *For* and *Against*. Use your answers from exercise 8 and your own ideas to explain your opinions to the other group. Think about these things:
- ecosystems and environment
- cost, quantity and quality of food

67

6 They've Got Talent!

Yes, you can!

1 Look at the photos and complete the words.

1 si__ __ing
2 da__c__ng 
3 __cti__g 
4 pl__ __ing music 
5 te__ __ing jokes 
6 wr__t__ng 

2 🔘 2.12 Robyn is making a film clip about TV talent shows. Read and listen to the information she finds about a new show. What is its name?

3 Choose the correct answer.

1 The new show is for _____ in Britain.
  a adults   b women   c teenagers
2 The TV audience and the people in the _____ watch the programme.
  a street   b studio   c theatre
3 The show's on TV _____ .
  a once a week   b once a month   c every day
4 They are having auditions _____ .
  a in London   b in New York
  c in different places in the UK
5 The winning act performs in front of _____ .
  a the audience   b the Queen
  c other teenagers

TEENS HAVE GOT TALENT

You too can make it!!
- Do you think you've got talent?
- Can you show your skills on national television?
- Can you impress the judges and our studio audience?
- Do you enjoy media attention?
- Are you looking for the chance to start a career in showbiz?

Millions of kids all over the world enjoy watching TV talent shows. But now you too can be in a show! Most young people can only dream of fame and fortune but now that fantasy is becoming a reality for hundreds of British teenagers.

Your big opportunity!
Why don't you audition for *Teens Have Got Talent*? What are you waiting for?
This show is for you, teenagers aged 13-19! Are you thinking, 'But I can't sing, I haven't got any talent'? Not true!! What about your other abilities? Can you dance? Can you tell jokes? Do magic? Write screenplays for television? Are you a composer or an actor? This is your chance to show us what you can do!

The acts we choose from the local auditions go on to perform on one of our weekly TV programmes. The judges and our TV audience then choose the best acts to go on to the final, and the winner performs in front of Her Majesty the Queen in our final Christmas Extravaganza!

4 Answer the questions.

1 How old are the participants in the new show?
2 Which talents are the producers interested in for the show?
3 Write five things you need to send to participate in the auditions.

FLASH FORWARD

What are your talents?

Singing, telling jokes...

68

GRAMMAR

can/can't

You too **can be** in the show!
But I **can't sing**, I haven't got talent!
Can you **dance**?

Find examples of *can* + verb in the text. Underline them.

5 Write sentences with *can/can't* using the prompts.

1. I / use a computer (✓)
2. you / dance (✗)
3. my brother / play the guitar (✗)
4. David and I / swim (✓)
5. my friends / do magic tricks (✗)
6. my mother / speak a foreign language (✗)

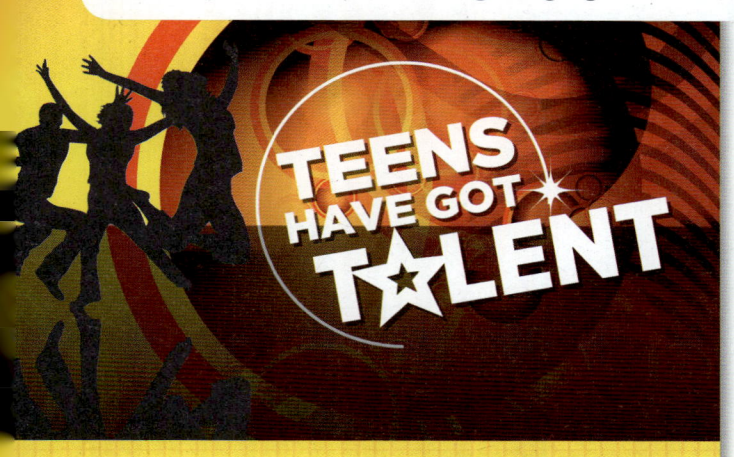

TEENS HAVE GOT TALENT

Why don't you come to an audition and try?
To participate in the auditions please send us:
- a recent photo
- a few words about you
- a brief description of your act
- a two-minute film clip of your act
- your email address and mobile number

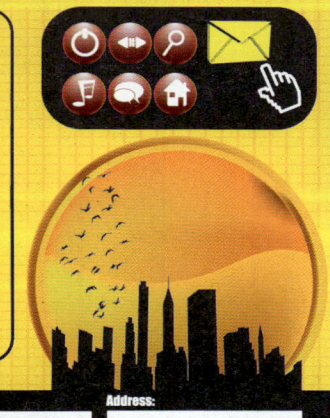

Vocabulary: Professions

6 🔊 2.13 Match the professions to the verbs, then listen and check.

1. actor/actress   a directs films
2. director   b uses a video or film camera
3. photographer   c paints pictures
4. cameraman   d acts in films
5. painter   f writes music
6. composer   g takes photographs
7. singer   h sings songs for an audience

7 Do you know what talents these people are famous for? Write their professions. Use the words from exercise 6 and other words for professions.

1 *Alicia Keys is a singer.*

Say it!

8 Think about things teenagers can do, for example, sports, games, hobbies. Ask four people in your class about their talents and abilities.

A *What sports can you play, Mark?*
B *I can play football and tennis.*
A *What else can you do?*
B *I can move my ears!*

9 Report back to the class about your classmates' abilities.

Mark can play tennis. Two people, Luke and Leonard, can play rugby...

6

I can dance quite well

1 🔘 **2.14** Listen and read. What is the situation?

☐ a lesson ☐ an exam ☐ an interview

Hannah Now, Anna, tell me about yourself.
Anna Sure. Err…
Hannah Let's start with films. Why do you want to come to the LAC?
Anna I love the cinema. It's magic. But I don't just want to watch films, I want to be in them!
Hannah Really? You want to be an actress then? And what about the Performing Arts? Can you dance?
Anna Yes, I can dance quite well. I go to modern dance classes on Wednesdays and Saturdays.
Hannah Good. You're a ballerina too! Can you play any musical instruments?
Anna No, I can't play music at all but I can sing really well. My singing teacher says I've got a great voice. At weekends I sing in a bar in Covent Garden with three friends. We've got a blues band.
Hannah What about languages? Can you speak any foreign languages?
Anna Yes, I can. I can speak French. And I'm learning Italian.
Hannah Really? Other interests or hobbies?
Anna I like making clothes and I enjoy taking photographs. I'm doing a photography course at the Arts Centre at the moment.
Hannah Excellent! Can you use a video camera?
Anna No, I can't, but I'm sure I can learn…
Hannah Right. Is there anything else you can do?
Anna Well… there's cooking. I'm good at cooking. I help in the kitchen of my parents' B&B.
Hannah Okay, cooking is creative. Let's write that too.

2 What things can Anna do? Write ✓, ✗ or ?

☐ dance
☐ play music
☐ sing
☐ speak another language
☐ use a digital camera
☐ use a video camera
☐ drive a car
☐ cook
☐ do magic
☐ write music

3 Answer the questions.
1. Why does Anna want to study at the LAC?
2. Anna is doing four courses at the moment. What are they?
3. What does she do at weekends? Where?
4. Write two of her hobbies.

FLASH FORWARD

What things from exercise 2 can your friends or the people in your family do? Write sentences.

My mum can play the piano. My friend can speak Russian.

6

Vocabulary: Hobbies and interests

4 🔘 **2.15** Write the expressions under the correct photos, then listen and check. Which of these hobbies do you like doing?

> play chess   chat online   listen to music
> collect cards   do motocross   go rollerblading
> make models   make clothes   play snooker

1 _____   2 _____   3 _____

4 _____   5 _____   6 _____

7 _____   8 _____   9 _____

I like playing chess but I don't like collecting cards.

GRAMMAR

Degrees of ability

I can't play music **at all**.
I can sing **really well**.

Find these expressions in the dialogue. What do they refer to, things or activities? Write them on the scale below.

> quite well   really well   not at all   well

0% ——— 50% ——— 100%

5 Which of the things that Anna mentions can you do? Can you do them *quite well, well, really well* or *not at all*? Write four sentences.

I can dance quite well.

FUNCTIONS

Talking about abilities and interests

Can you play any musical instruments?
No, I can't play music at all but I can sing really well.

Say it!

6 Look at the information about Antonio. In pairs, ask and answer about his abilities and interests. Use the expressions from exercise 2 and exercise 4.

LONDON ARTS CENTRE

Name: Antonio Clark
Age: 16   Nationality: British
Address: 12 Primrose Road, Liverpool
Languages: English, Italian (fluent), French (school)
Hobbies: photography, motocross, rollerblading, collecting international phone cards, listening to music, going to the cinema.
Film courses: I haven't got any real experience in the Performing Arts (I can't sing or dance) but I'm interested in making films. I did a two-week course in film-making at Bristol Film School and at the moment I'm taking an evening course in writing screenplays.

A *Can he sing?*
B *No, he can't.*

A *Can he speak a foreign language?*
B *Yes, he can speak Italian very well and French quite well.*

⚡ FLASHPOINT

I'm **good at** cooking.
Harry **is really bad at** singing!
I am **interested in** making films.

Write it!

7 Sell yourself! What are you good at? Write about your abilities and interests, the things you like. Can you do these activities well?

I can play the piano really well. I'm good at playing pop songs! I can't write screenplays but I'm interested in writing stories…

6 Vocabulary Workshop

Professions

1 Which people use these things? Match the objects to the professions.

1. ☐ actor
2. ☐ director
3. ☐ cameraman
4. ☐ photographer
5. ☐ painter
6. ☐ composer
7. ☐ singer

A B C D E F G

2 Match the part-time jobs for teenagers to the phrases.

1. A paper boy
2. A shop assistant
3. A pizza delivery boy
4. A babysitter

a. serves customers and sells things.
b. looks after children and plays with them.
c. rides a bicycle and delivers newspapers.
d. drives a motorbike and delivers pizzas.

3 🔘 2.16 Listen to a dialogue. What job is James having an interview for?

4 🔘 2.16 Now read the text and listen again. Which abilities does Mr Girotti says James needs for the job? Write them in the dialogue.

Mr Girotti	So, James, what can you do?
James	I'm good at basketball and I can play the guitar...
Mr Girotti	Yes but, err... for example, can you (1) _____ ? It's important for this job.
James	I can't drive a car but I can drive a scooter. I've got a Vespa.
Mr Girotti	Excellent! Now, do you know the town centre well? Can you (2) _____ easily?
James	Oh yes, I live in King Street – it's right in the centre. I know every street in town!
Mr Girotti	Fantastic! Are you good at (3) _____ ? You need to take the money and give change to customers when you deliver their pizzas.
James	No problem, I'm really good at maths. It's my favourite subject!
Mr Girotti	Great! Can you start tomorrow?
James	Yes, I can! Of course. Thanks!

5 Work in pairs. Choose one of the jobs from exercise 2. Student A is the manager and is interviewing student B. Student B answer student A's questions about his/her abilities and show him/her he/she is a good candidate for this job.

Hobbies and interests

6 Look at these words. Which are games and sports? Which are creative? Make a word web.

> play chess   collect cards   make models
> do motorcross   make clothes   go rollerblading
> play snooker   dance   sing   play an instrument
> do magic   cook   write music

Pronunciation: can/can't

When *can* is not stressed (*I can do it* or *Can you come?*) the vowel is weak, shown as /ə/. It can be strong and shown as /æ/ if we want to stress it and when it appears at the end of the sentence (*Of course you can!*). It is a strong vowel, shown as /ɑː/, in negative statements.

7 🔘 2.17 Listen and repeat these sentences.

1. Which sports can you play?
2. I can play the piano.
3. He can't swim.

8 🔘 2.18 Listen and repeat the words.

/æ/	/ɑː/
can, pan, Ann, hat	can't, plant, aunt, heart

9 🔘 2.19 Listen and write these words in the correct columns in the table in exercise 8.

> apple   start   bag   man
> tomato   car   banana   bat

10 🔘 2.20 Now listen, check your answers and repeat the words.

Spoken English

We use the expression *Really?* to express interest or surprise.

'I want to be in films.'   'I'm learning Italian.'
'**Really?**'   '**Really?**'

11 Work in pairs. Student A, make surprising statements about students in your class. Student B, express interest or surprise. Use the prompts from the list, or your own ideas.

> be Chinese   like Green Day
> speak Latin   play the trumpet
> have a pet snake   be twenty-five years old

A *Bruno is Chinese.*   B *Really?*

Flash on Grammar 6

can/can't

Affirmative			Negative		
I/You He/She/It We/You/They	can	dance.	I/You He/She/It We/You/They	can't (cannot)	dance.

Questions			Short answers
Can	I/you he/she/it we/you/they	dance?	Yes, I can./No, I can't.

We use *can*:
- to express ability or possibility:
  I *can* dance.   **I *can't* answer the phone.**
- to make requests:
  ***Can* you open the window please?**

📗 WB p. 48

1 Write sentences with *can/can't* using the prompts.

1 monkeys / write music (✗)
2 I / speak ten languages (✗)
3 dogs / swim (✓)
4 you / dance the tango (✗)
5 she / run 20 kilometres (✓)
6 I / sing in English (✓)

2 Make questions with *can* from these prompts, then write answers for them. Use short answers.

1 your teacher / speak English?
2 you / play the guitar?
3 you / close the door?
4 cats / swim?
5 your father / cook?
6 you / help me?

3 Which sentences in exercise 2 refer to ability and which refer to requests? Write R or A.

4 Make requests using the situations 1-10 and the expressions a-j.

1 It's hot.   a open the window
2 I don't have any money.   b watch TV
3 I can't speak Chinese.   c shout
4 I'm hungry.   d help me
5 I can't see.   e send an email
6 I'm thirsty.   f give money
7 I can't do my homework.   g speak English
8 I can't sleep.   h go to a restaurant
9 I can't hear you.   i switch on the light
10 My mobile isn't working.   j drink water

1 a It's hot./open the window
Can you open the window, please?

Degrees of ability

With *can* we sometimes use adverbial expressions like *well, quite well, really well, not at all* to express varying degrees of ability. They are always put after the verb and/or complement.

*I **can't** play the violin **at all**.*
*My brother **can** play chess **quite well**.*
*They **can** sing **really well**.*

📗 WB p. 48

5 Add adverbial expressions to make these sentences true for you.

1 I can break dance.
   I can break dance quite well.
2 I can act.
3 I can sing.
4 I can write stories.
5 I can play the guitar.
6 I can rollerblade.

good/bad at, interested in

To express a person's ability or interest we use the expressions *be good/bad at, be interested in* + noun or verb in *-ing*.

*I'm **good at** maths.*
*The boys **are good at** swimming.*
*You're **bad at** football!*
*Julia **is interested in** gardening.*

📗 WB p. 48

6 Complete the sentences with the correct form of *be good/bad, be interested*.

1 Italians _____ at cooking!
2 Dogs _____ at swimming.
3 _____ you _____ in coming with us to visit Redpath Castle tomorrow, Stewart?
4 I'm _____ at maths.
5 Wayne Rooney _____ at football.
6 Rihanna _____ at singing.
7 Keira Knightley _____ at acting.
8 My sister _____ in science or geography but she loves history. She says it's fascinating!

7 Complete the sentences with *good/bad at, interested in* to make them true for you.

1 I _____ maths.
2 I _____ sports.
3 I _____ drawing.
4 I _____ languages.
5 I _____ making friends.
6 I _____ finding solutions to problems.
7 I _____ making things with my hands.
8 I _____ playing a musical instrument.

6 Flash on Skills

The Commitments

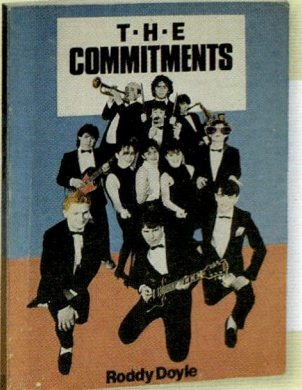

Before you read

1 Match the instruments to the photos.

1. ☐ guitar
2. ☐ piano
3. ☐ saxophone
4. ☐ bass guitar
5. ☐ trumpet
6. ☐ drums

The Commitments (1987) is a novel by Irish writer Roddy Doyle. It is the first story in *The Barrytown Trilogy* and is about a group of unemployed young people in the north part of Dublin. They get together to start a band.

A B C D E F

Reading

2 Read the summary of the plot of the book. What type of music do the Commitments play?

3 Now read the extract from the book. What does Jimmy ask the two boys to think about in relation to their band?

The plot

Two friends, Derek Scully and 'Outspan' Foster, decide to form a band but they soon realise that they don't know enough about the music business, so they ask an old friend from school, Jimmy Rabbitte, to be their manager. However, Jimmy believes the band should play soul music, not 'electronic pop'. He puts an advertisement in the local paper. It says, 'Have you got soul? Then Dublin's hardest working band is looking for you!' and The Commitments set out on a mission to bring soul to Dublin.

When Outspan and Derek decided that their group needed a new direction, they both thought of Jimmy. Jimmy knew what was new but wouldn't be for long and what was going to be new. Jimmy had Relax before anyone heard of *Frankie Goes to Hollywood*... Jimmy knew his music.

Jimmy speaks.
- Why exactly d'yis want to be in a group?
- Wha' d'yeh mean? Outspan asks.
He approves of Jimmy's question though. It's getting to what's bothering him and probably Derek too.
- Why are yis doin' it, buyin' the gear, rehearsin'? Why did yis form the group?
- Well...
- Money?
- No, said Outspan. – I mean it'd be nice. But I'm not in it for the money.
- The chicks?
- Jesus, Jimmy!
- No. says Derek.
- Why then?
- It's hard to say, says Outspan.
That's what Jimmy wants to hear. He jumps in.
- Yis want to be something different, isn't tha' it? Yis want to do somethin' with your lives, isn't tha' it?
- Sort of, says Outspan...
Jimmy is getting passionate now. The lads enjoy watching him.
- Yis want to get up there an' shout, I'm Outspan Foster! – He looks at Derek. – And, I'm Derek Scully! I'm not a loser! Isn't that right? That's why yis are doin' it. Amn't I right?
- I suppose yeh are, says Outspan.

(abridged and adapted text)

Literature 6

4 Answer the questions.
1. Why do Outspan and Derek contact Jimmy?
2. What is Jimmy good at?
3. What three reasons does Jimmy suggest for the boys forming their group?
4. What does he think is the reason to be in a band?
5. How do Outspan and Derek feel about his point of view?

5 The author tries to realistically represent the dialect of northern Dublin in the book. Answer these questions about the characters' use of language.
1. Find two words in the extract the characters use instead of *you*.
2. What happens to the ends of some words in this dialect? Give two examples from the dialogue.
3. Find these colloquial words in the text: *gear, loser, chicks*. What do you think they mean?

Listening

6 Before you listen, match the types of music to the bands or singers.

1	classical	a	Eminem
2	rap	b	Shakira
3	soul	c	Metallica
4	pop	d	Green Day
5	jazz	e	Luciano Pavarotti
6	heavy metal	f	Louis Armstrong
7	punk	g	Aretha Franklin

STUDY SKILLS
Listening for specific information

When you are listening for specific information it is not important to understand every word but to focus only on the parts which are relevant.

- Read the questions carefully and underline the key words you are looking for.
- On the first listening, note down the key words as you hear them. After listening, think about the topic that links these key words and make notes of any other words or phrases you know related to these.
- On the second listening, note down the other related words and phrases you hear in the context around the key words. Compare them to your previous notes.

7 🔊 2.21 Listen to the interview and write what the two young people do a) as a job, b) as a hobby. What words or phrases in the dialogue help you to identify this information?

8 🔊 2.21 Listen again. Read the statements and write T (true) or F (false).
1. Tom and Teresa are studying at university. ___
2. The Birds are a rap band. ___
3. The fans don't like the songs Jake writes. ___
4. The Birds have got three CDs in the shops. ___
5. They've also got a website. ___

9 🔊 2.21 Listen again and complete the information about the band The Birds.

The Birds are a new band from (1) _____.
Their favourite music is (2) _____ but they play (3) _____ too. Teresa is the (4) _____ and Tom plays the (5) _____ and he can also play the (6) _____ but he can't (7) _____!
Jake, the bass player, writes all their (8) _____ and he can also play the piano.

Speaking

10 Work in small groups. Imagine you are forming a band in your class. Which people can play instruments or sing? What are you and your friends good at? Talk about the people in your band.

A *Katie can play the violin.*
B *It's a rap band!*
C *Luke is good at playing the drums. He can be the drummer.*
A *OK. Robert can sing – he's got a nice voice...*

Writing

11 Write about your favourite band and the type of music they play. Think about these things.
- What type of music is it?
- Which band members play which instruments?
- What other things can they do (dance? act? write songs?)
- Why do you like their music?
- What are the names of some of their albums?

I really like Florence and the Machine. They play a mix of pop and punk and the words of their songs are really clever. There are five people in the band. Florence is the singer and she can play the guitar quite well too...

75

5 Flashback

GRAMMAR

some/any

1 Complete the dialogues with a/an, some/any.

A What do you have for breakfast?
B I have (0) *an* egg and some milk. And you?
A I have a cup of coffee and (1) _____ biscuits.
B My mum has (2) _____ fruit.
A Really?
B Yes, you know, (3) _____ apple and some orange juice.

A We don't have (4) _____ fruit at home.
B Really? Have we got (5) _____ bananas?
A No, let's do (6) _____ shopping.
B There isn't (7) _____ bacon in the fridge.
A But we've got (8) _____ cheese.
B And there's (9) _____ tomato.
A OK, let's go. Have you got (10) _____ money?

☐ 10

How much/many + quantities

2 Complete the sentences with much/many.

0 How *much* food is there in the fridge?
1 How _____ bacon have we got?
2 How _____ sugar do you want?
3 How _____ apples are there on the table?
4 How _____ eggs do you eat?
5 How _____ spaghetti is there in the cupboard?
6 How _____ pizza do you eat every week?

☐ 6

3 Complete the sentences with the phrases below. You can use them more than once.

> a lot   a little   a few   much   many

0 There aren't *many* pupils in class today: only three!
1 There are _____ of people in China: 1.3 billion.
2 There are too _____ eggs in this omelette. I can't eat it.
3 She has _____ of sugar in her tea, she likes sweet tea!
4 There isn't _____ sugar in her tea, she wants more.
5 He only has _____ sugar in his coffee. He doesn't like sweet things.
6 There are only _____ crackers in the packet, let's buy some more.
7 There are 100 biscuits in the tin, that's _____ !

☐ 7

4 Complete the chart with the correct quantifiers: *a few/a little*, *not much/not many*.

Quantifiers	Nouns
(0) *a few, not many*	eggs, sausages
(0) *a little, not much*	sugar, mile
(1)	potatoes, sardines
(2)	fish, water
(3)	biscuits, sweets
(4)	coke, orange juice
(5)	cake, pizza
(6)	crisps, mushrooms

☐ 12

can/can't

5 Write sentences with can/can't.

0 ride a bicycle (✗)   *He can't ride a bicycle.*
1 dance (✓) _____
2 sing (✗) _____
3 play the guitar (✓) _____
4 cook (✓) _____
5 swim (✗) _____

☐ 5

6 Write questions like the example.

0 speak French (you)   *Can you speak French?*
1 open the door (you) _____
2 close the window (we) _____
3 ride a horse (she) _____
4 cook (your grandfather) _____
5 help me please (you) _____

☐ 5

Degrees of ability

7 Look at the chart and complete the sentences with the words below (two answers may be possible).

100%			0%
really well	well	quite well	(not) at all

0 They play basketball *well/quite well* ; but they're a good team.
1 I speak Portuguese _____ because I am Brazilian!
2 Brazilians usually play football _____ – they're fantastic.
3 I'm not a fantastic musician, but I can play the guitar _____ . I'm not brilliant.
4 No, I can't dance _____ , I never dance.
5 She doesn't cook _____ . She always buys takeaway food.
6 Valerie can speak French _____ , but her German is much better.

☐ 6

76

Flashback 5 6

good/bad at, interested in

8 Complete the gaps with *good/bad*, *interested/not interested* and the correct form of the verbs below.

> use   go   ~~swim~~   climb   play   buy

0 Fish are *good at swimming* .
1 Cats are _____ at _____ trees.
2 Brazilians are _____ at _____ football.
3 I'm _____ in _____ this: how much is it?
4 I can't take good photos. I'm _____ at _____ a camera.
5 I'm _____ in _____ to the opera; it's boring.

☐ 5

Round up!

9 Underline the correct option.

A Mark, what do teenagers do in their free time?
B Well, we don't have (0) *much/many* free time. We have (1) *a lot of/a little* homework.
A Yes, but you have (2) *some/any* free time at weekends.
B (3) *A little/A few*, but not a lot.
A Do you have (4) *any/much* hobbies?
B I like taking photos.
A So you're interested (5) *in/at* photography. Are you very good (6) *at/in* it?
B I think I'm (7) *very well/quite good*. Not brilliant.

☐ 7

VOCABULARY
Food and drink

10 Complete the names of food.

0 bi *s c u i* ts
1 s_____ges
2 to_ _t
3 ba_ _n
4 ce_ _ _l
5 f_ _ _ _t ju_ _e
6 e_ _s
7 mu_ _ _ _ _ _ms
8 pa_t_ _ _s
9 b_ _ns

☐ 9

11 Complete the phrases with the words below.

> slice   ~~loaf~~   bag   tin   packet
> jar   bottle   carton   can

0 a *loaf* of bread
1 a _____ of biscuits
2 a _____ of milk
3 a _____ of coke
4 a _____ of cake
5 a _____ of jam
6 a _____ of potatoes
7 a _____ of water
8 a _____ of sardines

☐ 8

Professions

12 Complete the sentences with the correct words.

> actress   ~~director~~   photographer   painter
> composer   singers   paper boy   ~~cameraman~~

0 The film looks great – the *director* worked with a fantastic *cameraman* .
1 Michelangelo was a _____ .
2 Shakira and Andrea Bocelli are _____ .
3 Verdi wrote music: he was a _____ .
4 Tony takes newspapers to people's houses: he is a _____ .
5 John takes photos: he is a _____ .
6 Louise plays parts in films and in the theatre: she's an _____ .

☐ 6

FUNCTIONS
Talking about abilities and interests

13 Complete the interview.

> I have a few.   Have you got a lot?
> You're very good at taking photos.
> Have you got any photos with you?
> Yes, I have a lot of hobbies.   Yes, I take photographs.

A Do you have any hobbies?
B (1) _____ .
A Can you tell me about them?
B (2) _____ .
A You're a photographer? (3) _____ .
B Yes, I've got some photos in my bag.
A Thanks. (4) _____ . Brilliant.
B Thank you. I also collect stamps, you know.
A (5) _____ .
B No, I don't have many, (6) _____ , but they're very good ones.

☐ 6

14 Complete the second part of the interview with a word or phrase.

A (0) *Can* you use a computer?
B Yes, I can use a computer really (1) _____ .
A I see. Are you (2) _____ at music?
B Well, I (3) _____ play the guitar a little bit.
A Have you got (4) _____ experience in the other arts, painting, dance…?
B Well, I'm (5) _____ in painting but I (6) _____ understand modern art at (7) _____ . It's really difficult.
A A last question: (8) _____ write? Poems, screenplays…
B No, I'm afraid, I can't.

☐ 8

Total: 100

7 Love, Love, Love...

The Love Quiz

Vocabulary: Life events

1 🔊 2.22 Write these events from a person's life under the correct picture. Then listen and check your answers.

> have children   go to school   be born
> get married   find a job   retire

1 _____   2 _____   3 _____   4 _____   5 _____   6 _____

2 Read the quiz and put a tick (✓) on the correct answers.

'Love is like playing the piano. First you learn to play by the rules, then you forget the rules and play from your heart.'
Author Unknown

1 The annual festival for lovers is...
a Valentine's Day
b World Love Day
c St. Valerie's Day

2 Which actors were the two lovers in the film *Titanic*?
a Leonardo DiCaprio and Kate Winslet
b Nicole Kidman and Tom Cruise
c Antonio Banderas and Penelope Cruz

3 In which of these films were there two lovers, Bella Swan and Edward Cullen, with very long teeth?
a *Paranormal activities*
b *Zombie Flesh Eaters*
c *Twilight*

4 In the play *Romeo and Juliet* by William Shakespeare what happens to the two lovers?
a They get married.
b They never meet again.
c They die.

5 Which of these hit songs wasn't a love song?
a *Love the way you lie*, Rihanna
b *Holiday*, Green Day
c *Born to run*, Bruce Springsteen

6 The symbol of love in Celtic civilisation was...
a a bird
b a knot
c a heart

7 Which of these beautiful women was the cause of the Trojan War?
a Cleopatra
b Helen
c Beatrice

8 Can you complete these famous comments about love?

'All you need is _____.'
song by John Lennon & Paul McCartney

'Love means not ever having to say you're _____.'
Erich Segal in the novel 'Love Story'

3 🔊 2.23 Now listen to the Love Quiz and check your answers.

FLASH FORWARD

Can you correct these statements?
1 Bella Swan is a vampire in *Twilight*.
2 Romeo's lover was Kate Winslet.
3 The Trojan War was a war between the Trojans and the Italians.
4 John Lennon was a writer.

Vocabulary: Physical appearance

4 🔊 2.24 Read the descriptions of this famous couple and complete the table with adjectives for appearance, then listen and check.

> He's tall and slim with long, straight, blond hair and blue eyes. Sometimes he wears glasses.

> She's tall and slim too, and she's got long, straight, dark hair and big green eyes. She's very pretty.

eyes	brown, grey, black, _____ , _____
hair	fair, dark, red, grey, black, brown, curly, _____ , _____ , _____
height	short, _____
other	big, small, plump, plain, _____ , _____

5 🔊 2.25 Match these adjectives to their opposites, then listen and check.

1 plump   a dark
2 tall   b big
3 pretty   c slim
4 small   d short
5 fair   e plain
6 straight   f long
7 short   g curly

GRAMMAR

Past simple: *be*

Which actors **were** the two lovers in the film *Titanic*?
The symbol of love **was** a knot.

Find more examples of the verb *to be* in the Past simple in the quiz. Underline them.

⚡ FLASHPOINT

We use the past of the verb *be* + *born* to talk about a person's place and date of birth.

*Shakespeare **was born** in Stratford-upon-Avon.*
*You **were born** in the United States.*

6 Complete these sentences with *was, were, wasn't* or *weren't*.

1 You _were born_ in Turkey, is that right, Ronnie? In Ankara?
2 Leonardo DiCaprio _____ born in 1874. He _____ born in 1974.
3 The girls _____ at school in London, they were at school in Bristol.
4 Jennifer Aniston _____ Tom Cruise's wife, she _____ Brad Pitt's wife.
5 I _____ at school yesterday. I _____ at home because I was ill.
6 Romeo and Juliet _____ old in the play, they _____ two young lovers.

Say it!

7 In pairs, ask and answer about how your appearance is different now from when you were five years old.

A *Were you tall?*
B *No, I was short then... and plump!*
A *Was your hair brown?*
B *No, when I was a child my hair was blonde.*

7

Where were you last night?

1 🔊 **2.26** Listen and read. How does Anna's Dad feel? How does Anna feel?

Henry Where were you last night? You were late. It was after midnight…

Anna Well, it's a bit complicated. I was with my friends and…

Henry What about this morning? You were asleep until 10 o'clock. You can't stay in bed all morning! We need you in the kitchen. There were a lot of people at breakfast.

Anna Look, Dad, I'm 16 now…

Henry Yes, but you can't stay out till midnight! Were you in a bar? You're an intelligent girl, you know you can't go to bars at 16.

Anna I wasn't in a bar! I was at a pizza restaurant. Dad, give me a break!

Hilary What's going on you two?

Henry Anna was out last night and she wasn't here to help with the breakfast this morning! She's irresponsible!

Hilary Well, Henry, it was Anna's night off…

Anna And I'm not a little girl any more!

Hilary Now, now, Anna… You weren't here to clean the bedrooms yesterday either.

Anna I'm sorry Mum. I had an interview.

Henry An interview? For a job?!

Anna No, for the London Arts Centre. I want to be an actress!

2 Read the statements and write T (true) or F (false), then correct the false statements.

1. Anna was at home before midnight.
2. Anna was at a bar last night.
3. Anna usually helps with breakfast at the B&B.
4. Dad doesn't think Anna is serious about her work in the B&B.
5. Anna was out yesterday morning too.
6. Anna wants to go to the LAC.

3 Make questions from these prompts then ask your partner the questions. Are his/her answers correct?

1. be / Anna / at home / now?
   Is Anna at home now? Yes, she is.
2. be / dad / happy / today?
3. be / Anna / at a pizza restaurant / now?
4. be / Anna's mum / angry / with her?
5. be / Anna / 16?
6. be / Anna / an actress?

FLASH FORWARD

Where were you last night, at home or out with friends? Write about your evening.

I was at my friend Claire's house. We were in her room watching TV.

GRAMMAR

can for permission

You **can't** stay in bed all morning!
Can I go to the cinema with Caroline?

Find other examples of *can* for permission in the dialogue. Underline them.

4 Write requests for permission from the prompts below. Use *can*.

1 we / go to the swimming pool / afternoon?
   Can we go to the swimming pool this afternoon?
2 I / invite my friends / here / on Saturday night?
3 I / get / a scooter / for my birthday?
4 we / use / your computer / to go / on the Internet?
5 Susan / sleep / at our house / tonight?
6 I / have / a snack / please?

Vocabulary: Adjectives of personality

5 🔊 **2.27** Listen and repeat these words which describe personality. Which adjectives are positive and which are negative?

irresponsible silly intelligent friendly shy
talkative quiet reliable sensible responsible
polite calm funny nervous rude

Positive	Negative
intelligent,	irresponsible,

⚡ FLASHPOINT

We use the expression *be like* to talk/ask about someone's physical aspect or personality.
In the answer we only use *be + adjective*.

What's your new teacher like?
She's really nice!

What are your sisters like?
They're both small with black hair.

Say it!

6 Think of someone in your class. Can your partner guess who it is? Ask and answer.

A *Is it a boy or a girl?*
B *A boy.*
A *What's he like?*
B *He's polite and calm.*
A *Has he got dark hair?*
B *Yes.*
A *Mark?*

7 🔊 **2.28** Listen to the life of Marilyn Monroe and complete the Fact File.

Date of birth:	
Real name:	_____ Jeane Baker
First job:	in a _____
First roles:	small, she was in _____ (1949)
Prizes:	David di Donatello and the _____
Personality:	intelligent, _____, sweet and _____
Hair:	_____ but her real hair was _____
Husbands:	James Dougherty, a _____ officer; Joe DiMaggio, a _____ player; Arthur Miller, the famous _____

Say it!

8 In pairs, make and answer questions using these prompts.

1 what / be / her real name?
   A *What was her real name?*
   B *Her real name was Norma Jeane Baker.*
2 when / be / she / born?
3 what / be / her first job?
4 what / be / her first roles / in the cinema?
5 was / be / a good actress?
6 what / be / like?
7 who / be / her husbands?

Write it!

9 Write about a teacher or student you remember from your old school. Describe his/her appearance and personality.

Mrs Jackson was my History teacher at Primary school. She was tall and slim with brown hair. She was intelligent and friendly...

7 Vocabulary Workshop

Physical appearance

1 🔊 **2.29** Match the words to the parts of the face, then listen, check your answers and repeat the words.

- [ ] eye
- [ ] chin
- [ ] ear
- [ ] forehead
- [ ] nose
- [ ] mouth
- [ ] teeth
- [ ] cheek
- [ ] hair
- [ ] eyebrow

2 Which of these adjectives describe hair? Which describe physique? Write them in the correct groups then add any other words you know.

> tall   curly   slim   straight   wavy
> short   dark   plump   blonde

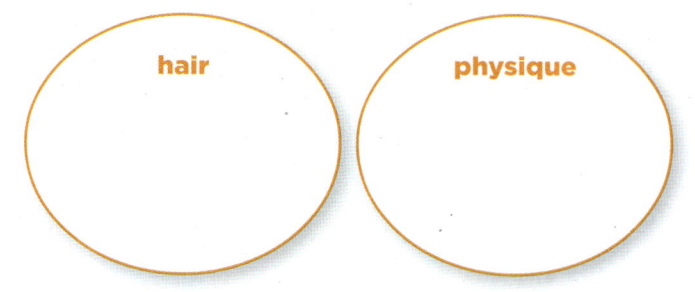

hair

physique

Adjectives of personality

3 Work in pairs. Play *The Minister's Cat*! Can you say an adjective of appearance or personality for each letter of the alphabet?

A *The minister's cat is an attractive cat.*
B *The minister's cat is a beautiful cat.*
A *The minister's cat is a clever cat...*

STUDY SKILLS
Making opposite adjectives

By adding the prefix *ir-*, *im-* or *un-* we can make the opposite of some adjectives.

responsible   irresponsible
happy   unhappy
polite   impolite

Pronunciation:
Stress on word prefixes

When we form opposite adjectives by adding the prefixes *ir-*, *im-*, *un-*, the main stress is on the syllable that is stressed in the 'original' adjective and the secondary stress is on the prefix.

4 🔊 **2.30** Listen and repeat.

responsible	irresponsible
polite	impolite
important	unimportant

5 Mark the stress on these adjectives.

1 relevant   4 responsive   7 rational
2 reliable   5 intelligent   8 attractive
3 practical   6 mature   9 perfect

6 🔊 **2.31** Now listen, check your answers and repeat the words.

7 🔊 **2.32** Now write and say the opposite of the adjectives in exercise 5, then listen, check your answers and repeat them.

1 _____   4 _____   7 _____
2 _____   5 _____   8 _____
3 _____   6 _____   9 _____

82

Flash on Grammar 7

Past simple: be

Affirmative			Negative		
I/He/She/It	was	happy.	I/He/She/It	wasn't	happy.
You/We/They	were		You/We/They	weren't	

Interrogative			Short answers
Was	I/he/she/it	happy?	Yes, I/he/she/it was. No, I/he/she/it wasn't.
Were	you/we/they		Yes, you/we/they were. No, you/we/they weren't.

We use *was/were* to describe situations in the past.

When I **was** at primary school I **was** short.
My mother **wasn't** born in Germany, she's Swiss.

Time expressions with the past

yesterday	yesterday morning/afternoon/evening
this morning/afternoon	on March 2nd/Monday
last week/month/year	three hours/days/months ago

WB p. 56

1 Write sentences with the Present simple and the Past simple of the verb *to be*.

1. Henry / at work / now / last night / in bed
   Henry is at work now. Last night he was in bed.
2. Maria / tired / now / last night / at a party
3. this year / they / France / last year / Greece
4. today / it / rainy / yesterday / sunny
5. this morning / I / fine / last night / ill
6. at the moment / we / at the beach / this morning / in the hotel

2 Complete the interview with the actress Beryl Stripe with the Past simple of the verb *to be*.

A (1) When *were* you born?
B I was born in July, 1980.
A (2) _____ you a good pupil at school?
B I (3) _____ very good in some subjects, especially English and history.
A (4) _____ you good at maths?
B No, I (5) _____ .
A Why (6) _____ you good at English but not at maths?
B My English and history teachers (7) _____ very good but my maths teacher was horrible.
A Why (8) _____ he horrible?
B The teacher was a woman and she (9) _____ very kind. She (10) _____ always angry, but very hard-working.
A What about you? (11) _____ you hard-working?
B No, I wasn't. I was a bit lazy.

3 Complete the sentences with the Past simple of the verb *to be*.

1. The film _____ very good, it _____ terrible. The actors _____ awful.
2. Our French teacher was very nice; she _____ friendly and the kids _____ afraid of her.
3. 'You _____ at home yesterday. Where were you?' 'No, I _____ at home. I _____ at the shops'.
4. The children _____ at school yesterday. They _____ at home, because yesterday was a holiday.

4 Work in pairs. Student A, choose one person, Student B, ask questions to guess who it is, then swap roles.

Leonardo da Vinci
I was born in 1452. I was an Italian artist and inventor.

John Lennon
I was born in 1940. I was an English singer and songwriter.

Albert Einstein
I was born in 1879. I was a German scientist.

Agatha Christie
I was born in 1890. I was an English novelist.

Charlie Chaplin
I was born in 1889. I was an English actor.

Marie Curie
I was born in 1867. I was a Polish physicist and chemist.

Elvis Presley
I was born in 1935. I was an American singer.

Walt Disney
I was born in 1901. I was an American film producer and director.

A *Were you a singer?* — B *Yes, I was.*
A *Were you American?* — B *No, I wasn't.*
A *Were you born in 1940?* — B *Yes, I was.*
A *Are you John Lennon?* — B *Yes, I am.*

can for permission

We use *can/can't* to ask for, give or refuse permission to do something.

Can I borrow the car, Dad?
Yes, you **can**./No, you **can't**.

WB p. 56

5 Complete the dialogue with *can/can't*.

Jane Mum, _____ I go out with my friends tonight?
Mum Tonight? But it's Tuesday, you've got school tomorrow. You know you _____ go out on school nights.
Jane Please, Mum! At the weekend the cinema is always too busy. _____ I go if we go to the early screening at half past five?
Mum Mmm. Well... you _____ go if you do all your homework before you go.

83

7 Flash on Skills

They're coming out of the kitchen...

Before you read

1 Look at the pictures. Do you know these famous British women? Why are they famous?

Reading

2 Read the paragraphs and check your answers to exercise 1, then complete the table.

name	born	died	profession
Elizabeth Tudor			
Florence Nightingale			

Elizabeth in Love

Elizabeth Tudor was born in 1533; she was the only child of King Henry VIII and his second wife, Anne Boleyn. The young Princess Elizabeth was an intelligent talkative child. She was a very good student: she was fluent in five languages but she was an excellent poet, musician and dancer, too. She also had a passion for horse riding. She was Queen of England from the age of 23.

She was a clever politician and a brilliant diplomat. She was also an enthusiastic patron of the arts. Her reign was the Golden Age of English culture: the economy was strong and London was full of great writers, musicians and painters.

Many young men were in love with this charismatic queen. However, she had a difficult personality. She was a flirt, but she was also rude and bad-tempered. The great loves of her life were the handsome Earl of Leicester and the charming Earl of Essex. But Elizabeth also had many suitors from the royal houses of Europe. However, at her death in 1603 at the age of 70, she was still unmarried.

Florence forever

Florence Nightingale was born in 1820 in Florence – her name comes from the name of the Italian city. Her family was rich and privileged but the idealistic Florence wasn't happy with her frivolous life in high society. For her, it wasn't a useful life and this quiet sensible girl had a secret ambition: her dream was to be a nurse.

She had a lot of friends and some close relationships with men but she was not interested in marriage: 'I don't want love and marriage to interfere with my career as a nurse'.

In the 1850s, the British were at war with the Russians and the newspapers were full of horrible stories about the terrible conditions for soldiers in military hospitals. There were hundreds of deaths every day. Florence, with help from her rich friends and other courageous doctors and nurses was able to help these soldiers. Thanks to Florence, the modern nursing profession was born.

Culture 7

3 Read the statements and write T (true) or F (false), then correct the false statements.

1 Elizabeth Tudor was from a big family. ___
2 Elizabeth was an old lady when she became Queen. ___
3 During Elizabeth's reign England was a very successful country. ___
4 Elizabeth married when she was seventy. ___
5 Florence Nightingale was from a very poor family. ___
6 Britain was at war with Germany in 1850. ___
7 The conditions for soldiers in the Crimea were excellent in the 1850s. ___
8 Florence and her friends were the first professional nurses in Britain. ___

4 What were the two women's personalities like? List the adjectives which describe them from the text, then look at their pictures and add some of your ideas.

Elizabeth Tudor was…
Florence Nightingale was…

Speaking

5 Test your memory! Student A, close your book. Student B, ask student A questions about one of the famous women from exercise 2. How much can he/she remember about that person?

A *When was Florence Nightingale born?*
B *Err, 1850?*
A *No, she was born in 1820.*

Listening

6 2.33 Listen to the information about another famous woman in history. Complete the information about her.

Name:
Nationality:
Born:
Died:
Profession:
Family:
Why famous:

7 2.33 Listen again and complete the paragraph about Pocahontas' work.

When she was a (1) _____ she was taken prisoner by (2) _____ soldiers. In prison she learned to speak (3) _____ and started to talk to the British about her (4) _____ and their (5) _____ , and to promote (6) _____ between the two countries… She was really the first Native American woman to work for better (7) _____ between white Europeans and (8) _____ minorities.

STUDY SKILLS
Writing a short biography

When you write a biography, first make notes about the dates of the main events in the person's life, then think about:

- where they were from and lived during their life
- what their profession was
- why they are famous now

Make a table like the one in exercise 2 and use it to organise your notes, then use the notes to write short complete sentences.

Writing

8 Use an internet search engine like Google to find information about one of these famous women and take notes. Read the tips in the Study Skills box then expand your notes to write a short biographical paragraph.

Queen Victoria

Charlotte Brontë

Elizabeth Fry

8 Out and About

A day out in London

1 Look at the photos. Do you know these places in London?

2 🎧 2.34 Michael, Antonio and Robyn visited some interesting places in London last week. Listen and read the extracts from Michael's email messages to his friend Luke. Match two photos to each of the three paragraphs.

1
This is a photo of our boat trip on the River Thames last Tuesday – it rained a bit but we enjoyed it – it was really relaxing and we saw a lot of famous places including the London Eye. At the end, we visited the Houses of Parliament. (That was a bit boring!) We wanted to visit Big Ben but it was closed to visitors.

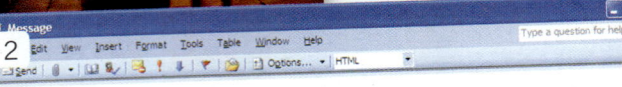

2
… We watched the ceremony of the Changing of the Guard outside Buckingham Palace last weekend. It took place at 11.30 and Antonio missed it because he arrived late! Then we went to the Tate Modern; it was an old power station but now it's an art gallery. It's really cool! The things there are weird but fascinating – I studied some of them in Art at school last term. We finished Sunday afternoon with some shopping in Oxford Street (zzzz!!) and Robyn bought some souvenirs.

3
Antonio wanted to go on a walking tour yesterday so we did the 'Mystery Walk'. We followed the trail of Jack the Ripper and we visited some places where famous crimes happened (but they weren't very frightening!). That part lasted two hours and was quite tiring. They also showed us the house of someone famous in Baker Street: the house is a museum now... Who lived there? I can't remember! Anyway, it was really interesting but we walked and walked. We were sooooo tired!

3 Read the statements and write T (true) or F (false), then correct the false statements.

1 The friends visited London by bus. ___
2 Michael liked the Tate Modern art gallery. ___
3 Antonio wanted to go shopping. ___
4 The Mystery Walk tour was very scary. ___
5 There is a cemetery in Baker Street. ___

4 When did the friends do these things?

1 Go on a boat trip?   *last Tuesday*
2 See the Changing of the Guard? ___
3 Go shopping in Oxford Street? ___
4 Go on a walking tour? ___

Vocabulary:
Adjectives in *-ing* and *-ed*

6 🔊 2.35 Complete the chart with the correct adjectives. Then listen and check.

It was...	I was...
boring	bored
tiring	tired
fascinating	_____
_____	frightened
interesting	_____
_____	excited
relaxing	_____

7 Write two captions for each picture. Use adjectives ending in *-ed* and *-ing*.

1 *She's relaxed.*
   The bath is relaxing.

2 _____

3 _____

4 _____

GRAMMAR

Past simple: affirmative

Regular verbs

It **rained** a bit but we **enjoyed** it.
Antonio **wanted** to go on a walking tour.

Find other examples of regular verbs in the Past simple in the text. Underline them.

Irregular verbs (for a full list see page 114)

come	*came*	do	_____
go	_____	see	_____
take	_____	buy	_____

Find the Past simple form of these irregular verbs in the text. Circle them.

5 Complete these sentences with the Past simple of the verbs in the box.

> ~~walk~~   visit   wait   watch   show   start   finish

1 We *walked* home yesterday because there were no buses.
2 The lesson _____ at 9 o'clock and _____ at 10 o'clock.
3 They _____ a Harry Potter film on Saturday.
4 You _____ your grandmother last weekend.
5 She _____ one hour for the bus; it was very late.
6 He _____ me his paintings.

Say it!

8 Work in pairs. Make dialogues using these prompts, past time expressions and appropriate adjectives from exercise 6.

1 watch TV / watch a DVD
2 play football / watch a football match
3 play computer games / clean the house
4 chat to friends / surf the Internet
5 visit an art gallery / go to the dentist's
6 play the guitar / work all day

A *I watched TV last night. What about you?*
B *I watched a DVD. It was interesting.*

8

What did you see in London?

1 🔊 2.36 **Listen and read. Where was Robyn this morning?**

Anna Hi! Did you enjoy your sightseeing this morning?
Robyn Oh, yes. I loved it. It was really interesting!
Anna Who did you go with?
Robyn I was with Antonio and Michael. Why didn't you come?
Anna Oh, I had stuff to do… Anyway, what did you see in London?
Robyn Well, we went to Buckingham Palace to see the Changing of the Guard.
Anna Oh no! Boring!!
Robyn No, it was cool. I took some great photos.
Anna Did you go to the Tate Modern?
Robyn Yes, we did. A bit boring.
Anna Oh, I think it's fascinating!
Robyn Anyway, the café was really amazing – great design. Then we did some shopping…
Anna What did you buy?
Robyn Well, Antonio bought some jeans and a T-shirt but Michael didn't buy anything.
Anna What about you?
Robyn I bought Big Ben, Buckingham Palace and a double-decker bus.
Anna Very funny, Robyn.
Robyn No really, look. I got them for my nephew. He's only eight! What about you? You look a bit upset!
Anna Actually I didn't have a good day. I feel depressed. I had another row with my dad.
Robyn What happened?
Anna Oh, he doesn't want me to go out, to see my friends, to go to the LAC…
Robyn You're kidding! Why not?
Anna It's a long story…

2 Complete with the correct name: Anna, Robyn, Antonio, or Michael.

1. _____ went sightseeing.
2. _____ didn't go sightseeing.
3. _____ went to Buckingham Palace.
4. _____ didn't see the Changing of the Guard.
5. _____ got some clothes.
6. _____ got some souvenirs.

FLASH FORWARD

What type of souvenirs do you like buying on holiday? Write some examples.

I like buying pens, …

Vocabulary: Emotions

3 🔊 2.37 Listen and repeat the adjectives. Then look at the photos and say how these things make you feel.

> embarrassed   jealous   angry   surprised
> worried   annoyed   happy   scared
> bored   upset   depressed   nervous

I feel upset/depressed when I have a row.

FUNCTIONS

Expressing feelings

What happened?
What's the matter?
You **look** a bit **upset**!

Actually I **feel depressed**.
I **was surprised**, it was really fun!

Say it!

4 Talk to your partner about how he/she feels today.

- A *You look a bit depressed. What's the matter?*
- B *Actually I feel a bit upset.*
- A *Why? What happened?*
- B *I got a bad mark in my Geography test.*

GRAMMAR

Past simple: negative and interrogative forms

Did you **enjoy** your trip round London yesterday?
We **didn't go** to the zoo, we went shopping.
What **did** you **see** in London?

Find other examples of these forms in the dialogue. Underline them.

5 Put the words in the correct order to make questions.

1. sightseeing / this morning / did / Anna / go?
2. Michael / did / this morning / Antonio / see?
3. did / go / with / Anna / her friends?
4. to / a / Robyn / museum / did / go?
5. did / any / souvenirs / Robyn / buy?

6 Swap notebooks with your partner and write answers to the questions in exercise 5.

7 🔊 2.38 Listen to Antonio talking about a London tour and complete the blanks in the leaflet.

TOUR 1: LITERARY LONDON
- Blackfriars: William Shakespeare (1) _____ a house here for £140.
- Sherlock Holmes' house in (2) _____ Street.
- Oscar Wilde's house in (3) _____.
- (4) _____ Dickens' house.
- Westminster Tube Station: scenes from the (5) _____ films.

Walks start at 10 a.m.

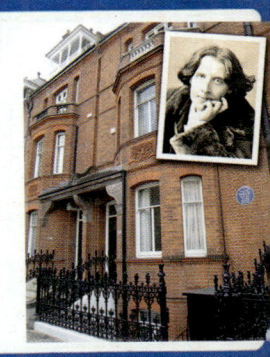

Say it!

8 Work in pairs. Use your completed notes to talk about the tour. What did you see? Where did you go? What happened there? Why are these places famous?

9 Talk about tour 2 in the same way.

TOUR 2: LONDON LEGENDS
- The church in the films *Four Weddings and a Funeral* and *Shakespeare in Love*.
- The Tower of London and Smithfields: the site of the execution of Sir William Wallace (*Braveheart*).
- Carnaby Street – the famous shopping street.
- The Beatles' music studios and the famous zebra crossing!

Walks start at 9 a.m.

8 Vocabulary Workshop

Adjectives in -ing and -ed

1 🔊 2.39 Write the adjectives in the correct group, then listen, check your answers and repeat the words.

> ~~boring/bored~~   interesting/interested
> exciting/excited   tiring/tired   relaxing/relaxed
> amusing/amused   annoying/annoyed
> worrying/worried   fascinating/fascinated

emotions
bored

things/events/people
boring

2 Add any other -ing or -ed adjectives that you know to the two groups in exercise 1.

3 Complete the sentences with the correct adjective. Underline it.
1 Our journey to India was *exciting/excited*.
2 Life in our village is really *boring/bored*.
3 I am *boring/bored*; let's play a computer game.
4 The film was *interesting/interested* but it was a bit long.
5 I can't do any work now; I am *tired/tiring*.
6 Her job is very *tiring/tired*.

STUDY SKILLS
Using a dictionary (2)

When you check a word in a bilingual dictionary always cross-check the different meanings listed in your language (if there is more than one) to find the most accurate translation for the word in the given context.

Emotions

4 Read the list of adjectives to describe emotions and translate them into your own language.

embarrassed	jealous	angry
surprised	worried	annoyed
happy	scared	bored
upset	depressed	nervous

5 Now check your answers in a bilingual dictionary?

6 Look at the pictures. How do the people feel? Write sentences.

1 _____ 2 _____ 3 _____ 4 _____

Pronunciation: Past simple -ed

The -ed ending on regular verbs is pronounced:
- /t/ when the base form of the verb ends with the sounds /f/, /k/, /p/, /s/, /ʃ/, /tʃ/
- /ɪd/ when it ends with a -d or a -t
- /d/ when it ends with all other sounds.

7 🔊 2.40 Listen and repeat the words.

/t/	/ɪd/	/d/
looked	visited	played
watched	ended	lived
_____	_____	_____

8 🔊 2.41 Write these words in the correct column in exercise 7, then listen, check your answers and repeat the words.

> walked   started   danced
> recorded   looked   showed

Spoken English: Use of *a bit*

We use *a bit* with words that have a negative sense to 'soften' them.

*You look **a bit** upset.*
*It was **a bit** complicated.*

9 🔊 2.42 Make these sentences 'softer' by adding *a bit* in the correct position, then listen and check your answers.

1 A I like Paris, but it's expensive.
  B And the French are unfriendly.
2 A Let's go for a pizza, I'm hungry.
  B Now? It's late.
3 A She wasn't very good at the interview.
  B No, but she was nervous and the questions were difficult.

Flash on Grammar 8

Past simple: regular verbs

Affirmative		Negative	
I/You He/She/It We/You/They	watched TV.	I/You He/She/It We/You/They	didn't watch TV.

Interrogative		Short answers
Did	I/you he/she/it we/you/they	watch TV?	Yes, I did. No, I didn't.

Spelling rules

- If the verb ends in *-e* we add *-d*:
  hope → hop**ed**

- If the verb ends in a consonant + *-y*, the *-y* becomes *-i* and we add *-ed*:
  study → stud**ied**
  but   play → play**ed**

- With some verbs we double the final consonant and add *-ed*:
  stop → stop**ped**
  travel → travel**led**
  prefer → prefer**red**

WB p. 64

1 Write the Past simple form of these regular verbs.

1 stay _____   6 marry _____
2 talk _____   7 listen _____
3 try _____   8 taste _____
4 travel _____ 9 plan _____
5 look _____   10 play _____

2 Complete these sentences with the correct past form of the verbs in the box.

> play   walk   visit   talk   enjoy   watch

1 They _____ for five kilometres. They were very tired!
2 Italy _____ very well in the match last night. They scored three goals.
3 We _____ the Louvre when we were in Paris. It was closed.
4 She _____ the tennis match online yesterday because her television is broken.
5 We _____ the party. It was boring.
6 I _____ to my mother on the phone every week when I was in Boston.

Past simple: irregular verbs

Many verbs have their own irregular form in the Past simple; we don't add *-ed*.

buy	bought	go	went
come	came	have	had
do	did	see	saw
drink	drank	make	made
eat	ate	write	wrote

WB p. 65

3 Use the Past simple of the verbs in brackets to complete the text.

Antonio (1) *went* (go) sightseeing yesterday but he (2) _____ (not go) with Anna. He (3) _____ (not see) the Changing of the Guard because he (4) _____ (get) there late. He (5) _____ (visit) Tate Modern. He also went shopping and (6) _____ (buy) some clothes. Anna (7) _____ (not go) sightseeing and she (8) _____ (not stay home). She (9) _____ (go) for an interview. When she (10) _____ (come) back home, she (11) _____ (have) a row with her dad.

4 Rewrite these sentences in the affirmative form. Make any other changes necessary to make logical sentences.

1 Oh no! We didn't buy any presents for Harry's birthday!
2 The twins didn't go to school today, they're not well.
3 I didn't make a lot of pasta. Are you very hungry?
4 Stewart didn't drink all the cola, there's some in the fridge.
5 Helen didn't see her history teacher today.
6 The package you're waiting for didn't come this morning.

5 Write questions from the prompts.

1 you / come to school / by bus / this morning?
2 you / have / a maths lesson / before your English lesson / today?
3 your family / live / in this town / when you were a baby?
4 you / like / the Harry Potter books / when you were small?
5 you and your friends / go / to the cinema / last weekend?
6 you / get / a lot of presents / for Christmas / last year?

6 Now swap with a partner and write answers to your partner's questions.

91

8 Flash on Skills

Victorian London

Before you read

1 Match the pictures to the words in bold in the text. Write the letters next to the words.

Reading

2 Read the text and try to complete it with the words from the box.

> aristocracy   black   capital   commerce   poverty   transport   roads   laws   food

In the 19th century Victorian London was an enormous, busy city. During the Industrial Revolution there was a lot of money in the (1) _____ but there were also a lot of problems with pollution, disease and (2) _____. In 1800 the population of London was around one million. After the invention of the **railway** ☐ it grew very quickly and by 1880 there were about 4.5 million people.

In the west of the city there were the fashionable areas like Regent Street and Oxford Street where the (3) _____ and the rich lived. In the east there were the docks and millions of London's poor. The **docks** ☐ were very important to the city's prosperity because at the time London was the centre of world (4) _____.

The streets of London were dark and dangerous in those times. Street cleaners cleaned the (5) _____ all day because they were always full of manure from the horses everyone used for (6) _____. The air in the city was often (7) _____ with smoke from the chimneys and at night it was very dark because there weren't any electric lights, only a few gas lamps.

Victorian London was a city of extremes with some very rich areas but also many very poor areas. There was a lot of social injustice and desperate people often ended their lives in prison or in the **workhouse** ☐. Here they had (8) _____ and a bed, but they worked very hard, didn't get any holidays, and didn't see their families. Charles Dickens wrote about the terrible conditions in these workhouses in his famous book *Oliver Twist*. The novel shocked the Victorian middle class and they asked the government to pass (9) _____ to reform the workhouses.

3 Match the two halves of the sentences.

1. Victorian London had
2. There were 4.5 million people
3. Regent Street was
4. There was a lot of horse
5. London didn't have electric
6. Many poor people
7. In the workhouses

a. manure in the streets of London.
b. light in Victorian times.
c. a lot of problems.
d. poor people lived in terrible conditions.
e. didn't have homes or food.
f. a fashionable area.
g. in London by the end of the 19th century.

4 Answer the questions.

1. What were the three main problems in London during the 19th century?
2. Who lived in the west of London?
3. Who lived in the east of the city?
4. Why were the docks so important to the city?
5. Why was it very dark in London at night?
6. Describe the conditions in the workhouses.

CLIL 8

Listening

5 🔊 2.43 You will hear a historian talking on the radio about *mudlarks*, *toshers* and *rivermen* in 19th century London. Listen. Which of these things are related to which jobs?

1 a long hook: _____
2 sewer tunnels: _____
3 coins and jewellery: _____

The mudlark   The tosher

6 🔊 2.43 Read the questions, listen again to the radio programme, then choose the correct answer. (✓)

1 What did the mudlarks do? They worked…
 a on boats on the River Thames.
 b near the River Thames.
 c on the mud of the River Thames.

2 What did mudlarks look for?
 a Coins, jewellery and old clothes.
 b Old shoes.
 c Fish.

3 What was it common to see on the River Thames in those days?
 a Men working.
 b Boats.
 c Dead bodies.

4 What did the rivermen do when the dead person's pockets were empty?
 a They threw the body back in the river.
 b They took the dead body to the police.
 c They took the body to the cemetery.

5 Where did toshers work?
 a In the sewers under the streets.
 b On the river Thames.
 c At the docks.

6 Why were they unpopular with their neighbours?
 a Because they were criminals.
 b Because they smelled terrible.
 c Because they were poor.

Speaking

7 Work in pairs. Find out about one of these unusual 19th century jobs and make some notes about it. Write questions to ask your partner about the job he/she chose and get ready to answer questions about your job.

   alewife   chimney sweep   blacksmith   cooper

A *Where did this person work?*
B *In rich people's houses.*
C *Did he make something?*
B *No, he cleaned something.*

STUDY SKILLS
Planning your writing

Before you start to write, try to make a list of all your ideas about the topic. This is a useful way to record any ideas that come into your mind without having to put them in any particular order at first. This is called 'brainstorming'. Later, you can choose those ideas which seem most relevant to the question you have to answer and you can just delete the others.

Writing

8 Work in small groups. What was your town like in the 19th century? How was it different then? Think about these things and make some notes:

- the different social classes
- where they lived (homes)
- the different areas of the city
- the jobs they did
- the lifestyle
- the fashions
- pollution and poverty
- life and teenagers

9 Write a short paragraph describing your town in the 19th century using your group's ideas from exercise 8. Try to include some real historical names for people, things or areas and any unusual information you can find about life then.

7 8 Flashback

GRAMMAR
Past simple: be

1 Complete with was/wasn't, were/weren't.

0 Michelangelo _was_ Italian.
1 Leonardo da Vinci _____ a pop singer.
2 Shakespeare _____ Greek.
3 Shakespeare _____ an English writer.
4 Romeo and Juliet _____ two lovers.
5 The Titanic _____ a famous train.
6 The Titanic _____ a big ship.

[6]

2 Complete the gaps with the correct form of the verb to be.

Police officer   Where (0) _were_ you at nine o'clock last night?
Robert   I (1) _____ with my friends.
Police officer   Where (2) _____ you with your friends?
Robert   I (3) _____ in a coffee bar.
Police officer   Who (4) _____ with you?
Robert   Simon and Claudia (5) _____ with me.
Police officer   Who (6) _____ Simon and Claudia?
Robert   They (7) _____ my best friends.
Police officer   (8) _____ they with you all evening?
Robert   Yes, we (9) _____ together all evening.
Police officer   (10) _____ Simon with you all evening?
Robert   Yes, he was.

[10]

3 Complete the short answers.

A Were you short?
B Yes, (0) _I was_ .
A Were you tall?
B No, (0) _I wasn't_ .
A Were you born in Argentina?
B No, (1) _____ .
A Were you born in Spain?
B Yes, (2) _____ .
A Were you a good pupil at school?
B Yes, (3) _____ .
A Were you happy at school?
B No, (4) _____ .
A Was your hair curly?
B No, (5) _____ .
A Were your teachers good?
B Yes, (6) _____ .
A Was your grandmother a songwriter?
B No, (7) _____ .
A Were your mum and dad politicians?
B No, (8) _____ .

[8]

Past simple: regular and irregular verbs

4 Write the correct form of the Past simple for these verbs.

0 listen   _listened_   5 try   _____
1 plan   _____   6 travel   _____
2 go   _____   7 buy   _____
3 drink   _____   8 write   _____
4 see   _____   9 eat   _____

[9]

5 Complete with the correct form of the verbs do or to be.

0 _Was_ Juliet sad? Yes, she _was_ .
0 _Did_ Shakespeare write plays? Yes, he _did_ .
1 _____ Romeo in love with Claudia? No, he _____ .
2 _____ Shakespeare an opera singer? No, he _____ .
3 _____ Magellan go round the world? Yes, he _____ .
4 _____ Romeo and Juliet maths teachers? No, they _____ .
5 _____ Van Gogh have a restaurant? No, he _____ .
6 _____ the Romans build good roads? Yes, they _____ .
7 _____ Monet and Van Gogh painters? Yes, they _____ .
8 _____ Leonardo da Vinci invent spaghetti? No, he _____ .

[16]

6 Complete the questions and answers with the correct form of the verbs below.

drink   eat   ~~buy~~   have   watch   play   go

0 Did he _buy_ a new MP3 on Saturday?
  No, he didn't. He _bought_ a new laptop.
1 Did you _____ spaghetti last night?
  Yes, I did. I _____ a lot of spaghetti yesterday.
2 Did you _____ an English test last week?
  No, we didn't. We didn't _____ an English test last week.
3 Did she _____ to the doctor on Wednesday?
  Yes, she did. She _____ to the doctor on Wednesday.
4 Did they _____ the film on TV?
  No, they didn't. They _____ the film on DVD.
5 Did your team _____ well in the match?
  Yes, they _____ very well.
6 Did the cat _____ all the milk?
  No, it didn't _____ all of it.

[12]

94

Flashback 7/8

Round up!

7 Complete these messages with the appropriate word or words.

Hi, Robert!
On Saturday I (0) _was_ with Paul. We (1) _____ to the cinema. We saw Laura and Martha. They (2) _____ with two guys. I (3) _____ know them. They (4) _____ English. I think they (5) _____ Spanish. They met on holiday in Ibiza… How are you?
Love,
Emma

Hi, Emma,
Thanks for your message. What film (6) _____ see? Was it the new vampire film? (7) _____ enjoy the film? Did Laura and Martha enjoy the film? (8) _____ scary? Were the two guys their boyfriends or (9) _____ just friends? I'm not jealous. I was just interested, that's all.
Love,
Robert

VOCABULARY
Physical appearance

8 Write parts of the face using the jumbled words.

0 hefadore _forehead_
1 hcni _____
2 tethe _____
3 owseyebr _____
4 rhia _____
5 eosn _____
6 ares _____
7 heeksc _____

Adjectives in -ing and -ed

9 Put in the correct -ing or -ed adjective of the verbs in brackets.

0 I stayed home and watched TV. It was very _relaxing_. (relax)
1 I wasn't anxious or worried. I was very _____. (relax)
2 The film was an action film. It was very _____. (excite)
3 I was very _____ about our trip to Paris. (excite)
4 The film was terrible. I was _____. (bore)
5 The book was very _____. I didn't finish it. (bore)
6 It was a vampire film. It was _____. (frighten)
7 It was a horror film but I wasn't _____ at all. (frighten)
8 I didn't go to the museum because I wasn't _____. (interest)
9 The show was very _____. (interest)

Emotions

10 Underline the correct emotion.

0 She hates flying in aeroplanes. She feels _happy/scared_.
1 You see your boyfriend/girlfriend with another boy or girl. You feel _bored/jealous_.
2 You passed a difficult test. You are very _surprised/angry_.
3 You get a lot of bad news. You feel _depressed/embarrassed_.
4 You had a row. You feel _upset/jealous_.
5 You don't want to sing a song in front of the class. You feel _embarrassed/bored_.

FUNCTIONS
Asking for permission

11 Ask for permission in these situations.

0 You want to go to a party on Saturday. Ask your mum for permission.
Mum, can I go to a party on Saturday?
1 It's hot in the room. You want to open the window. Ask your teacher.
2 Your friends Emma and Laura want to sleep at your house tonight. Ask your parents.
3 You want to use your friends computer for a couple of hours. Ask your friend.
4 You and your brother want to go to Berlin with the school. Ask your parents.

Expressing feelings

12 Complete the dialogue with the missing adjectives.

embarrassed   jealous   upset
annoyed   surprised   bored

A Why didn't you come to Laura's party?
B (0) I was _upset_.
A Why were you upset?
B Laura didn't ask me to come, she was (1) _____ with me because I went out with her boyfriend, Robert, and I think (2) she was _____.
A Well, of course she was jealous. Did she see you together?
B Yes and she was very (3) _____. She had no idea about me and Robert.
A How did you feel when she saw you with Robert?
B I was very (4) _____, I felt like a fool. An idiot. And now I'm very depressed. I am (5) _____ with Robert. I'm just not interested in him.

Total: 100

95

9 Is it Chance?

Genius! Or was it?

1 Do you know why the people in the pictures are famous? Match their remarks to the correct picture.

A — Isaac Newton
B — Archimedes 
C — Columbus 
D — William Webb Ellis  
E — Alexander Fleming

1 'I was at home in Syracuse. I was having a bath when I had a great idea!'

2 'It was a sunny day and I was sitting under an apple tree when an apple fell on my head and I discovered gravity.'

3 'I wasn't looking for 'America' – I was looking for India!'

4 'I wasn't trying to discover the world's first antibiotic. I was investigating bacteria in my laboratory when I discovered penicillin.'

5 'I was playing football with the other boys at school. The ball was coming towards me – I caught it and ran. That's how rugby started.'

SPORT | Rugby

Did you know that many of the great discoveries or inventions in history happened by accident or 'serendipity' – when you discover something while you are actually trying to do something else? They say that Isaac Newton, the father of modern physics, finally understood gravity, after years of research, when an apple fell on his head one day as he was sitting reading under a tree in his garden! And Christopher Columbus wasn't actually looking for it when he discovered America – he arrived there while he was searching for India!

One day, in 1823, the pupils at a famous school in Rugby, England, were playing in a football match. The game was in full swing and of course everyone was running and kicking the ball. Then one of the players broke the rules. William Webb Ellis was running when someone passed the ball to him, but Ellis didn't kick the ball, he jumped up and caught it in his hands! His opponents were chasing him but he ran like the wind with the ball in his hands until he got to the goal. The spectators were cheering wildly and everyone agreed that Ellis's controversial technique was incredibly exciting. The teams decided to make a new set of rules for a new ball game and rugby football was born.
Was this genius or serendipity?!

2 🔊 2.44 Now read and listen to the text. Which of the people from exercise 1 are mentioned in it?

3 Use the text and the quotes from exercise 1 to complete the chart.

Who	What was he doing?	What happened?
Archimedes	He was having a bath.	He had a great idea.
Columbus		
Newton		
Fleming		
William Ellis		

4 Answer the questions.
1 What school did Ellis go to?
2 What year was the famous football match?
3 What was the reaction of the spectators to Ellis's technique?
4 What did the teams decide after the match?

FLASH FORWARD

What did these famous people discover or invent? Write sentences.

Thomas Edison   Guglielmo Marconi
John Logie Baird

Vocabulary: Professions

5 🔊 2.45 Write the professions under the photos, then listen and check.

> engineer   secretary   electrician   scientist
> plumber   shop assistant   doctor   architect
> nurse   sailor   lawyer   postman

1 _____   2 _____   3 _____   4 _____   5 _____   6 _____

7 _____   8 _____   9 _____   10 _____   11 _____   12 _____

Say it!

6 What do the people in exercise 5 do in their professions? Describe one job to your partner. Can he/she guess which one it is?

A *This person designs houses and other buildings.*
B *An architect?*
A *Yes!*

GRAMMAR

Past continuous

An apple fell on his head one day as he **was sitting** reading under a tree.
Christopher Columbus discovered America while he **was** actually **searching** for India!

Find other examples of the Past continuous in the text and underline them.

7 Write sentences about the past. Use the Past continuous.

1 John sleep now / This time yesterday / Maths lesson
John is sleeping now. This time yesterday, John was having a Maths lesson.
2 they visit Paris now / This time last year / they / travel to Spain
3 at 8 o'clock this morning / Maria / have breakfast
4 at 9 o'clock yesterday / George / wait / for the bus
5 yesterday, at midday / Jenny / buy new clothes
6 this time last week / Jim / visit / the doctor

Say it!

8 Mary is a very efficient secretary. Look at her diary and say what things she was doing at these times yesterday.

> 8.00 a.m. – make coffee for sales meeting, book hotel in London for Mr Turner
> 10.00 a.m. – write letters to American clients, call sales department
> 11.30 a.m. – check email, edit sales brochure
> 1.00 p.m. – lunch with Sandra, food shopping at Fresco's
> 3.00 p.m. – interview new secretary Mr Mills, call Mr Turner for instructions about Friday
> 4.30 p.m. – send sales brochure corrections to Rosemary, book meeting room for Friday

At 8 o'clock she was making coffee for the sales meeting while she was booking Mr Turner's hotel.

Write it!

9 Write about what you were doing yesterday at these times.

> at 8 o'clock this morning   at 9 o'clock yesterday
> yesterday, at midday   this time last week
> at 10 p.m. yesterday   this time yesterday

This time yesterday, I was playing football.

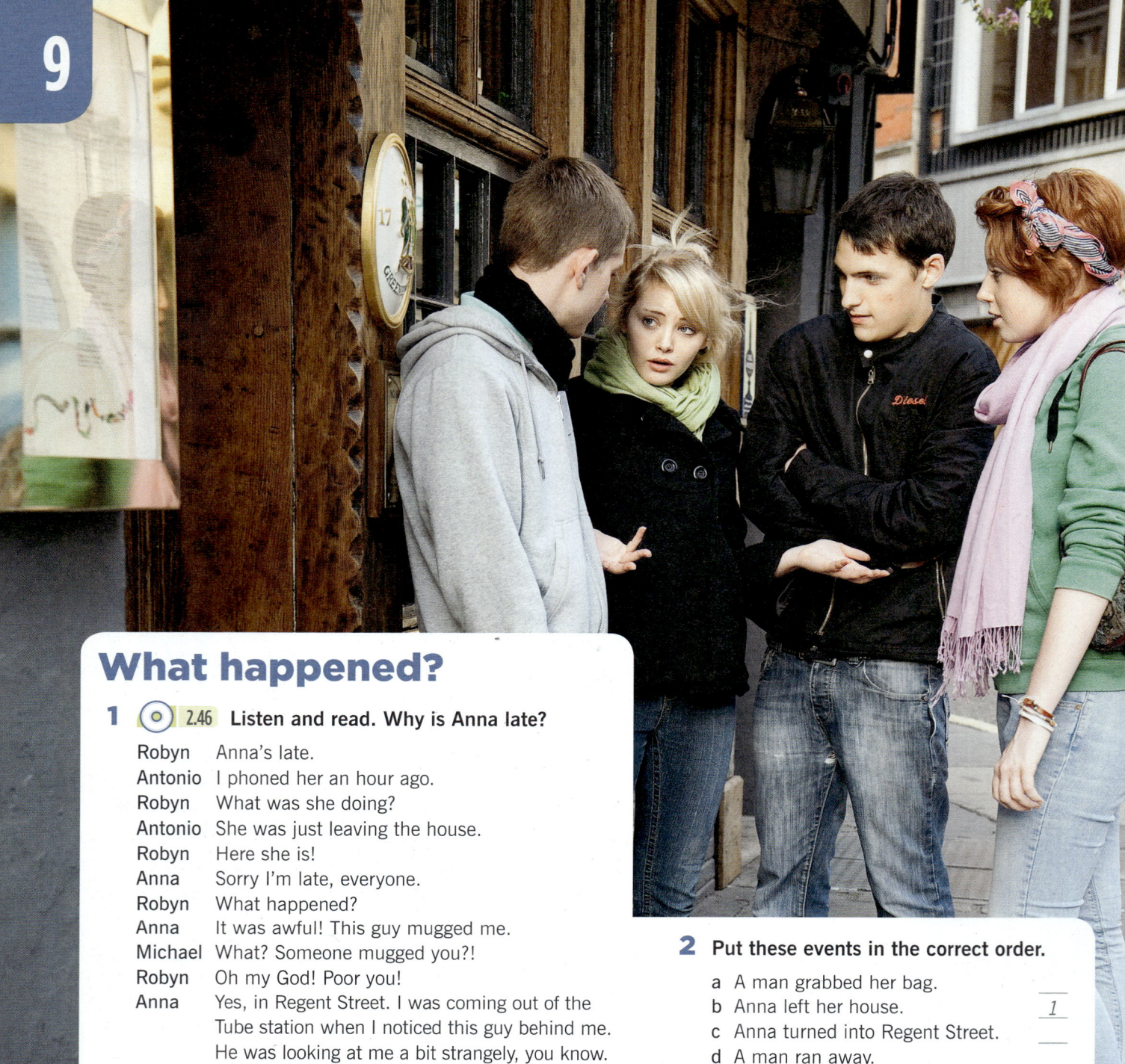

What happened?

1 🔊 **2.46** Listen and read. Why is Anna late?

Robyn Anna's late.
Antonio I phoned her an hour ago.
Robyn What was she doing?
Antonio She was just leaving the house.
Robyn Here she is!
Anna Sorry I'm late, everyone.
Robyn What happened?
Anna It was awful! This guy mugged me.
Michael What? Someone mugged you?!
Robyn Oh my God! Poor you!
Anna Yes, in Regent Street. I was coming out of the Tube station when I noticed this guy behind me. He was looking at me a bit strangely, you know. Then as I was turning into Regent Street, he came up behind me and said something quietly. I turned around and suddenly he grabbed my bag. While we were struggling I shouted for help and after that he ran away towards Piccadilly Circus.
Robyn Did you get a good look at him? Could you describe him to the police?
Anna I couldn't see his face very well, it was getting dark.
Antonio What was he wearing?
Anna He was wearing a black hoodie and jeans.
Michael Was he young?
Anna About 20 I think. He took my bag and my mobile, so I couldn't even phone for help.
Antonio Were you carrying much money?
Anna No, I wasn't. Just a few pounds. But I feel really shaken.
Robyn Of course you do! Come on, let's go in and sit down.

2 Put these events in the correct order.

   a A man grabbed her bag.
   b Anna left her house.   *1*
   c Anna turned into Regent Street.
   d A man ran away.
   e Anna met her friends.
   f Anna was in the Tube.
   g Anna came out of the Tube station.

3 Answer the questions.

   1 What did the man steal from Anna?
   2 Where did the mugging happen?
   3 What did Anna do?
   4 Where did the man go after he took the bag?
   5 What was in Anna's bag?

FLASH FORWARD

Imagine you are a witness to the crime. Describe Anna to the police. What was she wearing when it happened? What was she carrying?

9

GRAMMAR
Adverbs of manner

He was looking at me a bit **strangely**.

Find adverbs in the text to complete the second column in the table, then write the meanings.

Adjective	Adverb	Meaning
slow	*slowly*	_____
strange	_____	_____
quiet	_____	_____
sudden	_____	_____
good	_____	_____
real	_____	_____

4 Complete these sentences with the adverb from these adjectives.

> fast   loud   dangerous   quiet   clear   careful

1 We didn't hear the music, he was playing so _____ .
2 The lesson was difficult so we listened _____ .
3 They woke the baby up because they were talking _____ .
4 Try this paint – it dries very _____ .
5 Michael was driving very _____ that night and crashed his new Ferrari.
6 I don't understand her, she doesn't speak _____ .

Vocabulary: Crimes and criminals

5 🔊 2.47 **Match the words to the pictures, then listen, check your answers and repeat the words.**

> thief   robber   mugger   forger

1 _____   2 _____
3 _____   4 _____

FUNCTIONS
Talking about temporary events in the past

I was coming out of the Tube station **when** I noticed this guy behind me.
As I was turning into Regent Street, he came up.
While we were struggling I shouted for help.

6 Circle the time conjunctions in these sentences then complete them with the correct form of the verb, Past continuous or Past simple.

1 As we _____ (drive) along Rose Street we _____ (hear) a strange noise.
2 Where _____ you _____ (go) when I _____ (see) you yesterday?
3 They _____ (have) dinner when Sam _____ (arrive).
4 While Dianne _____ (eat) toffee she _____ (break) her tooth.
5 She _____ (read) the letter when she _____ (start) to cry.

Say it!

7 Look at the pictures and say what happened. Think about these things. Use the words and expressions which follow, or your own words.

- Where was the woman?   - What did he do?
- What was she doing?   - Where was the dog?
- Who arrived?

> have tea / favourite dog / man talk to woman /
> another man put bag behind chair /
> grab dog / leave / woman shout /
> men run away with dog / see tail stick out bag

Write it!

8 Now write the story of the dog thief. Use your notes and the time conjunctions from exercise 6.

99

9 Vocabulary Workshop

Professions

1 Make a word web for the words you know for jobs and professions. Use the categories below. Write the words for professions from unit 9 and 6 in the correct groups then add any other words you know.

- medical
- design/engineering
- financial/business
- **PROFESSIONS**
- retail/shops
- other
- services

STUDY SKILLS
Writing example sentences

Another way of recording new words is to write an example sentence in your notebook.

> *plumber* The plumber came to our house to fix the broken water pipes under the bath.
>
> *forger* The forger was very good and painted two exact copies of the Mona Lisa which no one recognised were false.

2 Write example sentences to illustrate the meanings of these jobs.

1. doctor
2. sailor
3. postman
4. electrician
5. shop assistant

Crimes and criminals

3 Complete the table with words about crime. Use a dictionary to check your answers.

Action	Crime	Criminal
to mug (a person)	mugging	_____
_____	forgery	_____
_____	_____	robber
to steal	theft	_____
_____	kidnapping	_____
to hi-jack (an aeroplane)	_____	_____

4 Match the crimes to their definitions.

1. mugging
2. robbery
3. forgery
4. theft

a. if you take something without the permission of the owner
b. if you take money or things from a bank or a shop especially using violence
c. if you attack someone and take their money
d. if you make an illegal copy of a document, a painting or money

Pronunciation: /ə/ (1)

As a general rule, unstressed vowels are pronounced with the weak schwa /ə/ vowel.

5 Say these words and circle the syllables with the /ə/ pronunciation.

1. doctor
2. photograph
3. sailor
4. America
5. secretary
6. cupboard
7. robber
8. water

6 🔊 2.48 Now listen, check your answers and repeat the words.

7 🔊 2.49 Listen and repeat these sentences and underline the syllables with the /ə/ pronunciation.

1. Look at the clock, it's a quarter to seven!
2. Remember to telephone your sister tomorrow.
3. Shall I send you another letter?
4. I was thinking about my wonderful trip to South America.

8 Write a list of the different vowels (letters) in exercises 5 and 7 which have the pronunciation /ə/.

Flash on Grammar 9

Past continuous

Affirmative			Negative		
I /He/She/It	was	doing.	I /He/She/It	wasn't	doing.
You/We/They	were		You/We/They	weren't	

Questions			Short answers
Was	I /he/she/it	doing?	Yes, I was./No, I wasn't.
Were	you/we/they		Yes, you were./No, you weren't.

We use the Past continuous to talk about actions that were in progress at a particular moment in the past.
*She **was having** breakfast at 8 o'clock this morning.*

We also use the Past continuous to describe a background action or one that was in progress and then interrupted by another shorter action expressed in the Past simple. Both actions are expressed in relation to each other with *when*, *as* or *while*.
*It **was getting** dark **when** we **arrived** at the hotel.*
***While** the baby **was sleeping**, she **prepared** dinner.*

📖 WB p. 72

1 Describe what you were doing in school yesterday at about 10 a.m. Use the words below.

1 we / study / history
   We weren't studying history.
2 teacher / write / on board
3 we / write / in our notebooks
4 I / talk / Paul
5 we / do / maths
6 outside / sun / shine

⚠ FLASHPOINT

Some verbs are not used in the continuous verb tenses, for example verbs of sensorial perception, emotion, will, mental state and possession:
*Stephen **wanted** a bike for Christmas but he **knew** it was impossible.*
*They **had** a summer house in Devon before the war.*
*I **smell** smoke: is there a fire?*

2 Complete the sentences with the verbs in brackets in the Past continuous or the Past simple.

1 I _____ (do) my homework in my bedroom when I _____ (hear) a noise.
2 We _____ (look) out of the window: it _____ (rain).
3 I _____ (talk) to Juana when it _____ (start) to rain.
4 We _____ (be) on holiday in France: the sun _____ (shine). It was beautiful.
5 I _____ (sit) on the train yesterday at 8 o'clock. I _____ (be/not) at home.

3 Write questions and answers using the prompts.

1 you do / your homework / lights went out? (read a book)
   A *Were you doing your homework when the lights went out?*
   B *No, I wasn't. I was reading a book.*
2 she read a book / the fire started? (watch TV)
3 you shop / lost your wallet? (go for a walk)
4 he drive carefully / he crashed? (drive very fast)

4 Read the paragraph and complete it with the correct tense of the verbs in brackets.

Birth of a hero
Bob Kane was sitting at his desk. He (1) _____ (look) for a good idea for a new hero. It was 1939, and everyone (2) _____ (read) *Superman*. At the time, Kane (3) _____ (read) a book about Leonardo da Vinci and his flying machine, the 'ornithopter'. He was feeling hot, so he got up and (4) _____ (open) the window. The moon (5) _____ (shine). He stood there, thinking. He (6) _____ (look) at the stars, when, suddenly, a strange object (7) _____ (fly) towards him and (8) _____ (crash) into the window. 'What was that? It was a bat. A bat! That's it! He was excited. 'I've got my hero', he said. Batman (9) _____ born.

Adverbs of manner

We use adverbs of manner to describe how an action takes place and they go after the verb they relate to and/or its complement.
*She drives **carefully**. He speaks English **quickly**.*

Many adverbs are formed by adding *-ly* to the adjective, but if the adjective ends in:
- **-y** the *-y* becomes *-i* and we add *-ly*:
  easy → eas**ily**
- **-le** the *-e* is dropped and we add *-y*:
  simple → simp**ly**

Irregular adverbs: *fast* → *fast*, *high* → *high*, *straight* → *straight*, *hard* → *hard*, *low* → *low*, *good* → *well*

📖 WB p. 72

5 Complete the following sentences with an appropriate adverb.

1 He played the piano *badly*. It was terrible.
2 He walked _____. He had an important meeting and he was late.
3 She sang very _____. She won a lot of prizes.
4 The waiter carried the plates _____. He didn't drop them.

9 Flash on Skills

Frankenstein's Monster

Before you read

1 *Frankenstein's Monster* is one of the most famous horror stories of all time. How much do you know about the story? Read the statements and write T (true) or F (false).

1. The author of the book was a teenage girl. ___
2. The author wrote the book in Italy. ___
3. Frankenstein is the name of a robot. ___
4. The monster was unhappy. ___
5. Frankenstein created a girlfriend for the monster. ___

2 Now read the background and plot information and check your answers to exercise 1.

Background

In 1816, 18-year old Mary Shelley and her husband the poet, Percy Shelley, were staying at the Villa Diodati, on Lake Geneva, with their friends, Lord Byron and John Polidori. They were reading a book of ghost stories one night, when suddenly Byron had an idea. 'Why don't we all write our own supernatural stories?' he suggested.
That night while Mary was sleeping, she had a dream about a scientist who created a monster. The idea grew in her mind and the next day she began writing her famous story: 'It was on a cold, dark night in November…'

The plot

Frankenstein's Monster is a novel in the Gothic horror tradition – dark, romantic and tragic. It tells the story of Victor Frankenstein, a young scientist. Frankenstein wants to create the perfect human being. He goes against the laws of Nature to create life using the bodies of dead men, but the thing he finally creates is a monster. The monster is lonely – he has no place in society – so he asks Frankenstein to create a companion for him. When at first he refuses, the monster is furious and decides to kill Frankenstein's family…

Reading

3 Read the three episodes from the story and match them with the pictures. Who is speaking in each paragraph, the monster or the scientist?

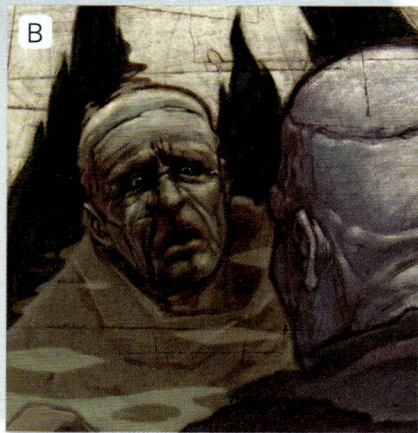

A

B

2
I was good, I looked for love and found only hate and fear. I didn't want to be bad. The hate and fear made me bad. No one saw good in me. Everyone saw bad in me because of my appearance. Everyone was afraid of me. But I was good; now I am a criminal. Now I really am bad. I can't believe I committed those crimes. Did I really kill those people? How did I become so evil? Dr. Frankenstein did not understand. I wanted love and friendship. But my crimes took me away from love. Am I the only criminal in this story?

C

1
It was a cold dark night in November. Outside, it was raining. The candle in my laboratory was slowly going out. The room was getting darker and darker.
In the bad light, I looked at the creature. Slowly, its eyes were opening. It was breathing. Its arms and legs were moving. I can't describe the thing… I wanted to make a beautiful creature but the monster was horrible; it had yellow skin, big muscles and black hair; his teeth were big and white; its eyes were grey and its lips were black. It was horrible, horrible. I ran out of the room.

Literature 9

4 Answer the questions.
1 Describe the scene on the night Frankenstein created the monster.
2 What did the monster look like?
3 Why do you think the scientist ran out of the room?
4 Why did the monster want to speak to the little boy?
5 Why did the boy cover his eyes?
6 Who was the boy?
7 Why did the monster become bad?
8 What did he want?

5 Read these words from the story and translate them into your own language.
1 evil   _____
2 bad   _____
3 good   _____
4 hate   _____
5 love   _____
6 fear   _____

Listening

6 🔊 2.50 Listen to a student talking about the book she read for her exam, *Frankenstein's Monster*. What does the girl say about the following things?
1 The main theme of the book.
2 The good character and the bad character.
3 The personality of Frankenstein.
4 The personality of the monster.

7 🔊 2.50 Listen again to what the student says about one of the themes of the story and complete the paragraph.

It's about _____ and _____ and what those words really _____ .
At first Frankenstein seems like the good guy and the _____ seems like the bad guy, but later we understand that Frankenstein is the _____ because he created the monster without thinking about the _____ .

3
I was sleeping in the woods when I saw a little child; he was coming towards me. He was young and I wanted him to be my friend. As he was passing me, I took his arm and pulled him towards me. 'Please don't be afraid,' I said. But he looked at me, covered his eyes and started screaming. 'Why are you screaming?', I said. 'Don't be afraid. I just want to speak to you'.
'Let me go, let me go', he shouted. He tried to run away.
'My father is an important man. He is Mr Frankenstein!'
'Frankenstein,' I said, surprised. 'He is my enemy. I hate him...'

Speaking

8 Work in small groups. Which of these themes do you think the story examines? (✓) Choose one and make notes of examples from the plot summary and story episodes in exercises 2 and 3.

☐ Humans can do anything if they try.
☐ Humans mustn't interfere with Nature.
☐ Money isn't important in life.
☐ Don't judge people by their appearance only.
☐ Family and friends are the most important thing in life.
☐ Love conquers all.

9 Choose a representative from your group to present your theme and the examples to support it to the class. Prepare some questions to ask other groups about the themes they chose. Think about:
- where the action happens
- the atmosphere the author creates for the events
- the development of the characters

STUDY SKILLS
Opening sentences

The opening sentence in a piece of narrative writing should get the reader's attention. A good opening sentence contains clues about the plot of the story and is intriguing so that the reader wants to read more.

'Last night I dreamed I went to *Manderley* again…'
(*Rebecca*, Daphne Du Maurier)

'It is a truth universally acknowledged, that a single man in possession of a large fortune must be in need of a wife…'
(*Pride and Prejudice*, Jane Austen)

Writing

10 Can you guess what Frankenstein is describing here? Rewrite the event in the third person and guess who committed the murder and why. Try to think of an intriguing opening sentence.

Those were the last moments of my life during which I enjoyed the feeling of happiness. On the first night of our honeymoon, in the garden of the inn, Elizabeth observed my agitation and asked, 'What is it, my dear Victor?'
'Oh! my love,' I replied, 'all will be safe; but this night is dreadful, very dreadful.' …
She left me, and I continued some time walking up and down, afraid of discovering the monster hidden somewhere in the grounds. But I discovered no trace of him and was beginning to relax when suddenly I heard a dreadful scream. I rushed into our room… She was there, lifeless and inanimate, thrown across the bed, her head hanging down and her pale features half covered by her hair.

103

10 Money

e-shopping

1 Match the different methods of shopping to the photos.

☐ online ☐ mail order ☐ markets ☐ shops ☐ vending machines

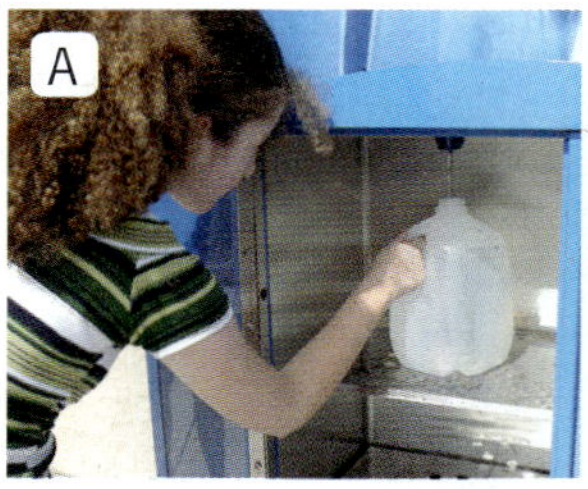

A | B | C | D | E

2 🎧 2.51 Listen and read the text extract. How many of the Frequently Asked Questions does it answer?

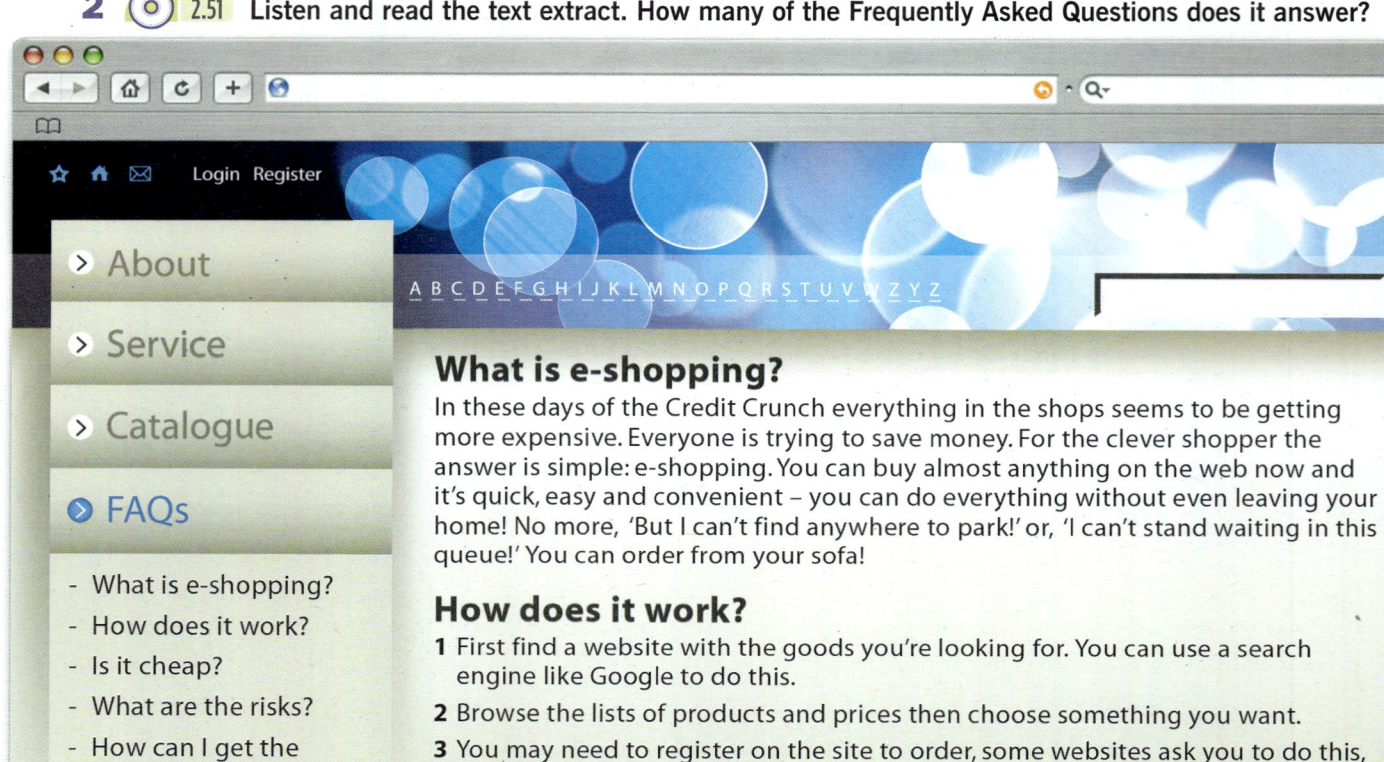

About

Service

Catalogue

› FAQs

- What is e-shopping?
- How does it work?
- Is it cheap?
- What are the risks?
- How can I get the goods to my home?
- Where can I find reliable online shopping sites?

What is e-shopping?
In these days of the Credit Crunch everything in the shops seems to be getting more expensive. Everyone is trying to save money. For the clever shopper the answer is simple: e-shopping. You can buy almost anything on the web now and it's quick, easy and convenient – you can do everything without even leaving your home! No more, 'But I can't find anywhere to park!' or, 'I can't stand waiting in this queue!' You can order from your sofa!

How does it work?
1 First find a website with the goods you're looking for. You can use a search engine like Google to do this.
2 Browse the lists of products and prices then choose something you want.
3 You may need to register on the site to order, some websites ask you to do this, some don't.
4 Complete the order form with the requested information about the type and quantity of goods you want, your delivery details and your credit card information. (Everyone needs a valid credit card or electronic payment card to pay for goods online.)
5 The company then sends you an email to confirm your order. Print it and put it somewhere safe – this is your receipt!

---

3 Read the statements and write T (true) or F (false).

1 e-shopping can help you to save money. ___
2 e-shopping is a bit complicated. ___
3 You need to register with any website to buy goods from it. ___
4 You can pay in cash when you shop online. ___
5 You get an electronic receipt when you shop online. ___

4 Write three advantages of online shopping that are mentioned in the text.

FLASH FORWARD

Are you an e-shopper? Do you know any e-shoppers? What do you/they buy online? What websites do you/they use?

I sometimes buy music online. I use iTunes or…

10

GRAMMAR

Compounds of *some, any, no, every*

Everything in the shops seems to be getting more expensive.
Is there **anyone** nowadays who isn't trying to save money?
Print it and put it **somewhere** safe.

Find other compound words in the text and underline them.

5 Complete the sentences with the words below.

> everything something somewhere somebody
> anything anywhere anybody nobody

1 At first, Laura didn't know _____ at her new school.
2 Paul didn't go _____ this summer, he stayed at home.
3 I've got _____ in this bag – can you guess what it is?
4 Switch the light on. I can't see _____ in here!
5 Sorry I didn't come to your party. _____ told me about it.
6 Last night, I saw _____ in our garden. I think he was a burglar.
7 I left my mobile _____ at school – I can't find it.
8 I don't know what to buy my mum for her birthday, she's got _____ !

Vocabulary: Shopping

6 🔘 **2.52** Match the words to the pictures, then listen and repeat the words.

> cash   credit card   cash card   cheque   voucher

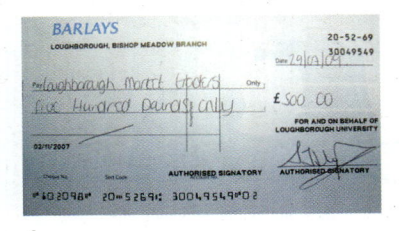

1 _____   2 _____   3 _____
4 _____   5 _____

7 Complete the third paragraph of the text using the words below.

> website   spend   price   pay
> bargains   costs   charge   goods

Is it cheap?

There are a lot of great (1) _bargains_ online because e-companies are less expensive – they don't have to pay rent for shops – they have a (2) _____ ; this means there's no one in the middle between them and you, the customer – no shops to run, no staff to (3) _____ – so they can keep their (4) _____ down and (5) _____ you less but still make a profit. You can compare the (6) _____ of the same (7) _____ between different suppliers easily and the Internet is also the place to find great second-hand bargains. On eBay you can really (8) _____ a lot less.

❗ FLASHPOINT

Cost can be a verb or a noun. *Price* can only be a noun.

How much does it **cost**? It's £5.50.
The **price** of the book online was $10.
The **cost**, with shipping, was $15.

Say it!

8 How much do these things cost in your city? Do you think they're expensive or cheap? Ask and answer questions with a partner.

> trainers   jeans   an MP3 player
> a pizza   a cinema ticket   a music CD

A *How much does a pair of jeans cost in your city?*
B *I think they cost about 80 euros in the shops.*
A *Wow! They're expensive!*

FUNCTIONS

Asking for information

How does it work?
What are the risks?
Where can I find reliable online shopping sites?

Write it!

9 Look back at the paragraph in exercise 7. Write five questions about it. Use the question words *what, why, where, how*.

10 Swap notebooks with a partner. Write the answers to his/her questions.

105

10 Whose is the chicken?

1 🎧 2.53 Listen and read. Which dish isn't for the three friends?

Waiter	Whose is the chicken?
Anna	It isn't mine – I'm having fish.
Waiter	Chicken with olives?
Michael	Err, no. It isn't mine. I'm having the vegetarian lasagne.
Waiter	Chicken for you, sir?
Antonio	No, steak. I don't think the chicken is ours. Maybe it's for someone at another table?
Waiter	Oh, I'm very sorry.
Michael	No problem.

five minutes later

Waiter	Whose is the fish? Anyone?
Antonio	It's hers, Anna's.
Waiter	And the vegetarian dish?
Anna	That's his. Michael!
Michael	Oh, thanks. It looks delicious!
Waiter	Is everyone having beer?
Anna	Err... no one wants beer, actually. Perhaps it's for the other table too?
Waiter	Oh, right. My apologies. Well, would you like anything to drink?
Anna	I'd like cola, please.
Antonio	And we'll have mineral water. Sparkling.
Anna	(*aside*) I haven't got any cutlery! Whose is this fork? Is it yours, Antonio?
Antonio	(*aside*) No, it's not mine. I haven't got any cutlery either!
Michael	(*aside*) Yeah, the food's good but the service is awful here!
Waiter	I'm sorry about the confusion, it's my first night.
Anna	Really? Don't worry about it, we're fine now.

2 Complete the three friends' orders.

Name	Food	Drinks
Anna		
Michael		
Antonio		

3 Answer the questions.

1 Where are the three friends?
2 Who ordered chicken with olives?
3 Which drinks do they ask for?
4 What is missing from the table?
5 Why is the service not very good?

FLASH FORWARD

Look at the words below. Connect them with *and* to make common expressions.

| bed | eggs | knife | hands | boys | salt | fish |

| fork | bacon | girls | pepper | chips | face | breakfast |

bed and breakfast

Vocabulary: At the restaurant

4 Look at the menu and the photos of some dishes, then write the names for the types of dishes.

desserts   side dishes
main courses   starters

starters	main courses	side dishes	desserts
Carrot and coriander soup	Chicken with olives and capers	Selection of grilled vegetables	Chocolate cake ....
Salmon paté	Grilled fish of the day	Roast potatoes	Apple pie ....
Mini herb omelette	Steak with wild mushrooms	Chips	Ice cream ....
		Green salad	

5 🔊 2.54 Listen to the dialogue in the restaurant. What do the girl and the boy order? Put a tick (✓) in the menu.

6 🔊 2.55 Match the words to the things on the table, then listen and check.

☐ knife ☐ fork ☐ spoon ☐ plate
☐ bowl ☐ cup ☐ saucer ☐ napkin
☐ glass ☐ salt and pepper

7 Complete the questions and answers with *whose* and possessive pronouns, then check your answers with the dialogue on page 106.

1 A _____ is this chicken?
  B It isn't _____ . I'm having the fish.
2 A _____ is the fish? Anyone?
  B It's _____ , Anna's.
3 A _____ is this fork? Is it _____ , Antonio?
  B No, it's not _____ . I haven't got any cutlery!

FUNCTIONS

Ordering in a restaurant

What would you like?
Would you like anything to drink?
Anything else?

I'd like cola, please.
We'll have mineral water.
Can I have the bill, please?
Can I pay by credit card?

GRAMMAR

Whose and possessive pronouns

Whose is the chicken?
It isn't **mine** – I'm having fish.
Whose is this fork? Is it **yours**, Antonio?

Find more examples of *whose* and possessive pronouns in the dialogue. Underline them.

Say it!

8 Work in groups of three. Student A, you are a waiter/waitress, take the customers' order. Student B and C, look at the menu in ex. 4, choose the things you want and order a meal.

10

107

10 Vocabulary Workshop

Shopping

1 How can you pay when you use these methods of shopping? Complete the sentences.

1 When you shop in a supermarket you can pay by _cash_ , _____ or _____ .
2 When you shop at a vending machine you can usually only pay by _____ .
3 When you shop online you can pay by _____ or with a gift _____ .
4 When you shop by mail order you can pay by _____ or _____ .
5 When you shop at a market you can pay by _____ .

2 Which of these words are nouns and which verbs? Write N (noun) or V (verb).

1 bargain   _N_
2 charge   ____
3 cost   ____
4 goods   ____
5 items   ____
6 price   ____
7 save   ____
8 spend   ____
9 pay   ____
10 cheque   ____

At the restaurant

3 Complete the menu with two appropriate dishes in each section.

Bell's Diner
Starters   Main courses   Side dishes   Desserts

4 What do we use the things in the box below for? Match these five definitions to the correct words, then write your own definitions for the other five.

> knife   fork   spoon   plate   bowl   cup
> saucer   napkin   glass   salt and pepper

1 You use it to drink tea or coffee. _____
2 You use it to cut your food. _____
3 You use it to eat soup or desserts. _____
4 You use it to clean your mouth after a meal. _____
5 You use it under a cup. _____

5 What do these words mean? Write definitions for them, then check your answers in a dictionary.

> tablecloth   teapot   milk jug   sugar bowl

Pronunciation: /ə/ (2)

The vowel sound of the *schwa* /ə/ is always found in monosyllabic words or in unstressed syllables.

6 🔊 2.56 Listen and repeat the sentences.

I want to take you to the library later.
(I want tə take you tə the librəry latə.)

Can I have a glass of water?
(Cən I have ə glass əf watə?)

7 Underline the words with one syllable which are pronounced /ə/ in these sentences.

1 Is the butcher's next to the fish and chip shop?
2 She got out of bed and started to pack her bags.
3 Let's go to the seaside on Saturday!
4 Where did you put that pair of brown shoes?

8 🔊 2.57 Now listen, check your answers, then repeat the sentences.

Spoken English: Apologising

I'm very sorry.
No problem.

Perhaps it's for the other table?
Oh right. **My apologies.**
Don't worry about it.

9 Complete the mini-dialogues with expressions from the box.

1 A Have you got my keys please, Jane?
   B Oh, _____ I left them at home.
   A _____ There are some other keys in the garage.

2 A Excuse me, we booked a family room but the room we've got is a double room.
   B Oh, _____ , sir. Let's see if there's a family room free for you.

10 Work in pairs. Choose one of the situations below. Student A, apologise to your partner, Student B accept his apology.

1 You can't go to your partner's party on Friday.
2 You lost your partner's dog in the park.
3 You forgot to bring your partner's homework to school.

Flash on Grammar 10

Compounds of *some, any, no, every*

	people	things	places
some	somebody/someone	something	somewhere
any	anybody/anyone	anything	anywhere
no	nobody/no one	nothing	nowhere
every	everybody/everyone	everything	everywhere

- We use compounds of *some* in affirmative sentences.
  There's **someone** in the garden.
- We use compounds of *any* in negative sentences and in questions.
  Do you know **anybody** in Australia?
  No, I don't know **anyone**.
- We use compounds of *no* in a negative sentence with an affirmative verb.
  There's **nothing** in this bag!

📖 WB p. 80

1 Complete the sentences with compounds of *some, any, no* or *every*.

1 A What did you do at school today?
  B _____ . Our teacher was ill.
2 A What did the history teacher say?
  B She said _____ about the Renaissance. I didn't understand _____ .
3 A Where do you want to go in the summer?
  B _____ with a lot of sunshine!
4 A Who did your sister marry?
  B _____ with a lot of money!
5 A Who was at the party?
  B _____ ! All of my friends – it was fantastic.
6 A Who did you go out with?
  B _____ . I was alone.

2 Choose the correct answer.

1 Listen! There's *no one/someone/everyone* at the door.
2 There's *anything/something/everything* wrong with my mobile phone – it doesn't work.
3 What happened? There's water *nowhere/somewhere/everywhere*.

Possessive pronouns

I	you	he	she	we	they
my	your	his	her	our	their
mine	yours	his	hers	ours	theirs

📖 WB p. 80

Whose...?

We use the question word *whose* to ask about possession. It can be followed by the verb *to be* or by a noun.

Whose bag is this, Dan?
It's my bag, it's **mine**.
Whose are these shoes?
They're **ours**.

📖 WB p. 81

3 Underline the correct word in each sentence.

1 It's *my/mine* fork. It's not *your/yours*.
2 This is *my/mine* camera. It's not *her/hers*.
3 That's not *our/ours* table. This is *ours/our*.
4 *My/Mine* bag is expensive. *Your/Yours* is cheap.
5 *Who/Whose* is this chicken? It's *mine/my*.
6 *What/Whose* is this pasta? It's *yours/your*.
7 *What/Whose* is this? It's *his/him*.

4 Complete the dialogue with possessive pronouns.

Mum Boys, this room is a terrible mess! Whose is this sports bag? Neil, is it (1) _____ ?
Neil Yes Mum, it's (2) _____ .
Mum Put it in the cupboard, please. And whose are these shoes? Jamie's?
Neil Yes, they're (3) _____ .
Mum Jamie, take your shoes downstairs. Are these the computer games Leo gave you?
Neil No, they're (4) _____ . These are (5) _____ and those are Jamie's.
Mum Well, don't leave them on the floor!

like and *would like*

- We use *like* + verb in *-ing* to talk about likes and dislikes.
  I like read**ing**.
- We use *would like* to say what we desire in a polite way and we use the expression *Would you like...?* for invitations and offers. It can be followed by a verb in the infinitive form or by a noun.
  I'd like some mineral water, please.
  Would you **like to go** out with me?

📖 WB p. 81

5 Complete the sentences with *like* or *would like*.

1 Good evening sir. What _____ you like to drink?
2 _____ you _____ Susan? I think she's a bit boring.
3 _____ they _____ to come to the theatre with us?
4 I _____ your new shoes – they're really cool!
5 Peter _____ (not) _____ dogs. He's scared of them.

109

10 Flash on Skills

Pocket money

Before you read

1 Read these sayings about money and match them to the explanations.

1 Money doesn't grow on trees.
2 The love of money is the root of all evil.
3 Money talks.
4 Never marry for money but marry where money is.
5 Time is money.

a Don't waste time when you are working.
b Don't marry a person just because they are rich, but find someone who isn't poor.
c It isn't easy to find, or make, money.
d Too much materialism causes problems for people.
e If you have a lot of money you have more influence over other people.

Reading

2 Read the text about pocket money. Choose the best title for it from the English sayings in exercise 1.

Title: _____

Home
News
Support
Contact us
FAQs
Blog

FAQs (Frequently Asked Questions)

What is pocket money?
Pocket money is a small amount of money that parents give their children regularly. It's theirs to manage and spend as they want. Sometimes people in the family (for example, grandparents) give kids money for birthdays or other special days too.

When do kids get it?
Kids in Britain get pocket money from their parents every week or every month. Families don't usually just give money to their kids when they want it. They think this spoils kids.

How much pocket money do British kids get?
That depends. How much can the parents afford? How many kids are there in the family? How old are the kids? Some parents pay kids for doing jobs in the house or for doing the shopping. Many families in Britain start bank accounts for their kids so they can start to save money when they are young. Each family is different.

Why is pocket money a good thing?
Parents believe managing their pocket money helps kids learn about the value of money and encourages them to save for things they really want. Some people also get their children to do work in the home in exchange for pocket money to teach them that money comes from working, you don't get it for nothing!

What kids say...

'I do 5 jobs (like gardening and washing the car) every week for my dad to get pocket money.'
Brian, 15

'I don't do jobs in the house but my parents give me 5 pounds a week to spend.'
Jenny, 14

'I get twenty pounds every two weeks – ten pounds of that is for jobs I do in the house for my mum. I wash the dishes, clean the house and babysit for my brother. I usually put 5 pounds in the bank and spend 15 pounds on stuff I need.'
Maggie, 15

Culture 10

3 Read the statements and write T (true) or F (false), then correct the false statements.
1. Pocket money is money you receive from family members for your birthday. ___
2. Most kids get their pocket money every day. ___
3. British parents don't think it's good to give children money when they ask for it. ___
4. Many British children have bank accounts to help them save their money. ___
5. All British parents give their children pocket money in exchange for work they do in the home. ___

4 Answer the questions.
1. How much money do teenagers get for their pocket money?
2. What sort of jobs do they often do in exchange for pocket money?
3. What percentage of her pocket money does Maggie save?

Listening

5 🔊 2.58 Listen to a radio presenter talking to some British teenagers about how they spend their pocket money and complete the table.

	Sophie	Hannah	Rajit
Where does the money come from?			
How much money does he/she get?			
What does he/she spend the money on?			

Speaking

6 Underline the three things that you spend most of your money on.

- clothes and accessories
- sweets, chocolate, snacks
- computer games
- magazines
- sporting events
- cinema
- other entertainment
- books
- mobile phone credit
- music CDs or downloads
- DVDs
- other

7 Compare your answers with other students in your class. Ask and answer questions with four other students about your spending habits.
A *How much money do you get every month?*
B *About 40 euros.*
A *Do you spend it on clothes?*
B *No, I usually spend a lot of it on credit for my mobile phone and music downloads from the Internet.*

Writing

8 Use the information you found out to make a pie chart about your class's spending habits. What are the four most popular things students buy? Calculate the percentages and divide the pie chart into 4 triangles, plus one for the 'Other' category. Colour, then label the 5 triangles.

Our spending habits class 1B

STUDY SKILLS
Annotating visual information

Sometimes you may be asked to annotate visual images or graphic information with labels and captions. These can help the reader to understand the information presented better. The language we use for these is short and factual and it isn't always necessary to write full sentences. It's important that the notes are positioned next to the information they explain on the page.

The most common types of annotations are: titles, labels, captions, keys, footnotes.

9 Now annotate the pie chart you made in exercise 8. Think about where to put the different types of information. Remember to specify these things:
- the title of the pie chart
- the source of your information
- what types of goods are represented by the coloured triangles
- the percentage of the total represented by each triangle

9 Flashback

GRAMMAR
Past continuous

1 Complete these sentences with the past continuous form of the verbs in brackets.

0 I _was having_ lunch at 2 o'clock. (have)
1 The sun _____ when we got to the park. (shine)
2 It _____ when we left the park. (rain)
3 He _____ on his mobile phone during the lesson. (talk)
4 Yesterday, at 10 o'clock, we _____ a history test. (have)
5 They _____ breakfast when someone knocked on the door. (have)
6 No, I _____ to music on my MP3, I _____ to the radio. (listen)
7 No, they _____ to the airport, they _____ to the station. (go)
8 No, Paul _____ (listen) to the teacher, he _____ (look) out of the window.

☐ 11

2 Complete with the past continuous form.

0 A Was he playing basketball on Saturday morning?
   B No, he _wasn't_. He _was playing football_. (play football)
1 A Were you having lunch when I called you?
   B No, we _____. We _____ TV. (watch)
2 A _____ a lot on the phone? (I/talk)
   B Yes, you _____. You _____ for one hour!
3 A _____ to school when they saw the old man? (they/walk)
   B Yes, they _____. They _____ to school. (go)
4 A _____ (she/wear) a blue coat when she left the house?
   B No, _____. She _____ a red coat. (wear)

☐ 11

3 Underline the correct verb.

0 I _was drinking_/drank coffee, when my phone rang.
1 We had/were having a house near the school, when I was a kid.
2 She walked/was walking in the park, when it started to rain.
3 I was reading a book in bed, when I heard/was hearing a noise.
4 The children wanted/were wanting to go skiing at Christmas.
5 We weren't having/didn't have lunch at 3 o'clock, we were drinking coffee.
6 They ran/were running out of the building, when the fire started.

☐ 6

Adverbs of manner

4 Underline the correct answer.

0 He wasn't driving simply/slowly when he crashed the car. He was driving at 100 kilometres per hour.
1 She explains maths very good/well. Everyone understands.
2 She's a great athlete. She can jump very hard/high.
3 She works very fast/easy. She always finishes first.
4 Walk quick/straight on and turn left at the corner of the street.
5 The teacher explains everything very simply/hard. She doesn't use difficult words.

☐ 5

Compounds of *some, any, no, every*

5 Choose the correct word: *a*, *b* or *c*.

0 I understood _everything_ the French woman said. My French is perfect!
   a nothing   b something   c everything ✓
1 I can see _____ standing by our car. What does he want?
   a someone   b anyone   c anybody
2 There is water _____ on the floor! You left the tap on all night!
   a nowhere   b somewhere   c everywhere
3 Do you write to _____ in English?
   a anybody   b no one   c anything
4 I've got _____ in my bag. Look, it's empty.
   a everything   b something   c nothing
5 She didn't know _____ about Tibet before she went there.
   a anything   b anyone   c somebody
6 I can't find my bag _____. Where is it?
   a somewhere   b anywhere   c everywhere

☐ 6

Whose and possessive pronouns

6 Complete the gaps with the correct possessive pronoun.

0 Those are my shoes. They're _mine_.
1 This book belongs to Peter and Paul. It's _____.
2 The blue bike is Martha's. It's _____.
3 The house in Washington belongs to me and my wife. It's _____.
4 It's not your pen, it's John's. It's _____.
5 That's my seat, not your seat. It's _____.
6 This is your pullover. It's _____.

☐ 6

Flashback 9 10

Round up!

7 Underline the correct word in this dialogue.

Mum   Laura! (0) *Whose/Who* are those books on the floor?
Laura (1) *My/Mine*, Mum. Sorry! I forgot them.
Mum   Well, pick them up! (2) *Nobody/Everybody* in this house makes a mess; (3) *nothing/nobody* helps me tidy up.
Laura But Mum, I (4) *did/was doing* my homework. I was working really (5) *fast/hard*.
Mum   Look, you can leave your things (6) *anywhere/nowhere* – but not on the living room floor.
Laura Mum, I was just (7) *go/going* to take them to my bedroom!
Mum   OK, then, (8) *where/whose* are these socks on the chair?
Laura They're not (9) *hers/mine*, Mum. I think they're (10) *your/yours*.
Mum   (11) *My/Mine*? Oops, sorry, Laura.

[11]

VOCABULARY
Professions

8 Complete the names of professions.

0 s c i e n t i st
1 d _ _ or
2 la _ _ _ r
3 n _ _ se
4 ar _ _ _ _ _ ct
5 se _ _ _ _ _ ry
6 sa _ _ _ _ r
7 en _ _ _ _ _ _ r
8 pl _ _ _ _ r
9 po _ _ _ an
10 el _ _ _ _ _ _ _ ian
11 s _ _ _ as _ _ _ _ _ nt

[11]

Crimes and criminals, Shopping

9 Choose the correct word in these sentences.

0 I was on the bus, when somebody *stole/mugged* my bag.
1 She was walking alone at night, when some *muggers/kidnappers* took her mobile.
2 She *forged/hijacked* a passport and used a new name.
3 Bank *robberies/robs* are very common nowadays.
4 Can I pay with my *credit card/goods*?
5 They don't accept cheques or cards you have to pay *cash/costs*.
6 There are a lot of great *bargains/vouchers* online.
7 I got this coat very cheap. I *saved/spent* a lot of money.
8 How much did they *charge/cost* you for the drinks?

[8]

FUNCTIONS
Talking about temporary events in the past

10 Unscramble the dialogue.

☐ OK. And what about yesterday?
☐ As I was going into the bank, a strange thing happened.
☐ I was waking up! I always wake up at about eight.
☐ Did you see a robbery?
☐ Why? Where were you going? Were you going to school?
[1] What were you doing at eight o'clock this morning?
☐ At eight o'clock yesterday I was waiting for the bus.
☐ No, I wasn't. I was going to the bank. I had to get some money.
[12] And the wind was blowing and it was beginning to rain...
☐ Really! Oh no!
☐ No, but a tall man was coming out of the bank with a big bag of money and as he was getting into his car, he dropped the bag and all the money fell onto the pavement.
☐ And what happened?

[10]

Ordering in a restaurant

11 Complete the dialogue in a restaurant. Write one or two words in each gap.

A Are you ready to (0) *order*?
B Yes, we are.
A What (1) _____ like?
B I'd (2) _____ an omelette and chips, please.
A (3) _____ like something to drink?
B Yes, please, (4) _____ like some orange juice.
A Would you like (5) _____ else?
B No, (6) _____ all, thank you.
A And you, sir?
C I'd (7) _____ chicken, please.
A Chicken; you can have rice (8) _____ chips with your chicken; which (9) _____ like?
C I'd like (10) _____ rice please, thank you.
A Anything (11) _____ ?
C Yes, I'll (12) _____ some mineral water. By the way, (13) _____ we pay by credit (14) _____ ?
A Yes, (15) _____ .

[15]

Total: [100]

Appendix

Irregular verbs

Base form	Past simple	Past participle	It means...
be	was/were	been	
become	became	become	
begin	began	begun	
bet	bet	bet	
bite	bit	bitten	
blow	blew	blown	
break	broke	broken	
bring	brought	brought	
build	built	built	
burn	burnt/burned	burnt/burned	
buy	bought	bought	
catch	caught	caught	
choose	chose	chosen	
come	came	come	
cost	cost	cost	
cut	cut	cut	
deal	dealt	dealt	
dig	dug	dug	
do	did	done	
draw	drew	drawn	
dream	dreamt/dreamed	dreamt/dreamed	
drink	drank	drunk	
drive	drove	driven	
eat	ate	eaten	
fall	fell	fallen	
feed	fed	fed	
feel	felt	felt	
fight	fought	fought	
find	found	found	
fly	flew	flown	
forget	forgot	forgotten	
get	got	got	
give	gave	given	
go	went	been/gone	
grow	grew	grown	
hang	hung	hung	
have	had	had	
hear	heard	heard	
hide	hid	hidden	
hit	hit	hit	
hold	held	held	
hurt	hurt	hurt	
keep	kept	kept	
know	knew	known	
learn	learnt/learned	learnt/learned	
leave	left	left	

Base form	Past simple	Past participle	It means...
lend	lent	lent	
let	let	let	
lie	lay	lain	
light	lit	lit	
lose	lost	lost	
make	made	made	
mean	meant	meant	
meet	met	met	
pay	paid	paid	
put	put	put	
read	read /red/	read /red/	
ride	rode	ridden	
ring	rang	rung	
run	ran	run	
say	said	said	
see	saw	seen	
sell	sold	sold	
send	sent	sent	
set	set	set	
shoot	shot	shot	
show	showed	shown	
sing	sang	sung	
sink	sank	sunk	
sit	sat	sat	
sleep	slept	slept	
smell	smelt/smelled	smelt/smelled	
speak	spoke	spoken	
spell	spelt	spelt	
spend	spent	spent	
spill	spilt	spilt	
stand	stood	stood	
steal	stole	stolen	
stick	stuck	stuck	
sweep	swept	swept	
swim	swam	swum	
take	took	taken	
teach	taught	taught	
tear	tore	torn	
tell	told	told	
think	thought	thought	
throw	threw	thrown	
understand	understood	understood	
wake	woke	woken	
wear	wore	worn	
win	won	won	
write	wrote	written	

Phonetic alphabet

Consonants		Vowels and diphthongs	
Symbol	Example	Symbol	Example
p	pen	iː	eat
b	board	ɪ	it
t	table	e	bed
d	day	æ	has
k	cap	ɑː	start
g	go	ɒ	hot
f	funny	ɔː	door
v	very	ʊ	book
θ	think	uː	moon
ð	mother	ʌ	love
s	sunny	ɜː	skirt
z	zoo, his	ə	the
ʃ	she	eɪ	day
ʒ	measure	əʊ	know
h	hungry	aɪ	five
tʃ	cheese	aʊ	sound
dʒ	joy	ɪə	hear
m	my	eə	hair
n	nobody	ʊə	pure
ŋ	sing		
w	water		
l	look		
r	read		
j	young		

English punctuation

A	CAPITAL LETTER
a	lower case
.	full stop
,	comma
'	apostrophe
;	semicolon
:	colon
?	question mark
!	exclamation mark
-	hyphen
—	dash
…	dots
/	slash
' '	quotation
" "	double quotation marks
( )	brackets

Appendix 10

Audioscripts

1.02

Antonio	Hi, I'm Antonio Clark. I'm 16 years old and I'm from Liverpool.
Michael	Hello! My name's Michael Winters. I'm 16 and I'm from Manchester.
Anna	Hi, I'm Anna, Anna Harrison. I'm 16. I'm from London.
Robyn	Hello, my name's Robyn MacGregor. I'm 16 years old and I'm from Edinburgh.

1.03

Paolo	Hello, I'm Paolo.
Monica	Hi, my name's Monica.

1.04

Luca	Paolo, this is Monica.
Monica	Hi, Paolo. Nice to meet you.
Paolo	Hello, Monica.

1.05

A Hi, how are you?
B I'm fine thanks. And you?
A I'm OK.

1.06

Robert Hi, I'm Robert and I'm from England. She's Kristen and she's from the USA. We're actors. What about you?

1.07

America – American
Australia – Australian
Belgium – Belgian
Britain – British
Brazil – Brazilian
Canada – Canadian
China – Chinese
Colombia – Colombian
Croatia – Croatian

Finland – Finnish
Germany – German
Ireland – Irish
Italy – Italian
Japan – Japanese
Portugal – Portuguese
Scotland – Scottish
Spain – Spanish
Turkey – Turkish

1.08

Sweden – Swedish
Norway – Norwegian
Russia – Russian
Switzerland – Swiss
Holland – Dutch

Poland – Polish
The Czech Republic – Czech
Slovakia – Slovakian
Romania – Romanian
Malta – Maltese

1.09

A Hi, where are you now? Are you out?
B No, I'm not. I'm in my bedroom. Where are you?
A I'm on the bus.
B Where's Laura?
A She's at home.
B Where are your mum and dad?
A They're at work.
B Is Paolo with you?
A No, he's not.

1.10

A What's your name?
B Javier Bardem.
A Are you from Argentina?
B No, I'm not.
A Where are you from?
B I'm from Spain.
A Ah, you're Spanish.
B Yes, I am. And you? What's your name?
A I'm Julia Roberts.
B Are you from Canada?
A No, I'm not.
B Where are you from?
A I'm from the USA.
B Ah, you're American.

1.11

1 It's black and red: Albania.
2 It's yellow and blue: Sweden.
3 It's red, white and blue: USA.
4 It's blue, white and yellow: Argentina.
5 It's black, yellow and red: Belgium.
6 It's green, white and orange: Ireland.
7 It's blue, yellow, red, white and green: The Seychelles.
8 It's yellow, orange and white: Bhutan.
9 It's black, red and orange: Germany.
10 It's yellow, green, orange and purple: Sri Lanka.

1.12

a b c d e f g h i j k l m n o p q r s t u v w x y z

1.13

Official	Have you got a laptop?
Passenger	No, I haven't. But I've got an MP3.
Official	Have you got liquids, water or shampoo in your bag?
Passenger	Yes, I have…

1.14

1 camera
2 wallet
3 MP3 player
4 watch
5 laptop
6 comb
7 iPod
8 sunglasses
9 mobile

1.15

baby – babies
child – children
tooth – teeth
foot – feet
shoe – shoes
man – men

woman – women
box – boxes
person – people
mouse – mice
watch – watches

1.16

Mamie Gummer is an actress. Her mother is Meryl Streep, the famous actress. Her father is Don Gummer. She has got two sisters, Louise and Grace Gummer; Grace is also an actress. Her brother is Henry, a singer and songwriter.

Jack Henry Robbins is an actor. He is from a family of actors and musicians. He is the son of two famous stars. His father's name is Tim Robbins, the actor and his mother is Susan Sarandon, the actress. Jack Henry's grandfather, Gil, is a musician. His grandmother, Mary, is an actress. Jack Henry has got a brother, Miles Robbins. He's a singer in a rock band. He's got a half-sister, Eva Amurri. Eva is an actress and she's the daughter of an Italian director, Franco Amurri, and Susan Sarandon. His aunt, Tim Robbins' sister, Adele, is an actress. His uncle, David Robbins, Tim Robbins' brother, is a musician.

Audioscripts

1.17
1. Miles is Jack Henry's brother.
2. Don Gummer is Meryl Streep's husband.
3. Susan Sarandon is Eva Amurri's mother.
4. Adele is Tim Robbin's sister.
5. Adele is Jack Henry's aunt.
6. Jack Henry is Adele's nephew.
7. Meryl is Don's wife.
8. Jack Henry is Gil's grandson.
9. Mary is Jack Henry's grandmother.
10. Gil is Miles' grandfather.

1.18
A Rod, this is Laura.
B Hi, Laura. I'm Rod.
C Nice to meet you.
B Nice to meet you, too. What class are you in?
C I'm in class 10A.
B Yeah? My cousin is in that class!
C What's his name?
B She's a girl. Her name's Julie Macintosh.
C Julie Macintosh? She's nice.

1.19
1. locker
2. whiteboard
3. bin
4. pencil case
5. desk
6. board pen
7. textbook
8. notebook
9. sharpener
10. pencil
11. eraser
12. folder

1.20
1. Stand up.
2. Sit down.
3. Put your hands up.
4. Open your books!
5. Close your books.
6. Open your bags.
7. Close your bags.
8. Put your left hand up.
9. Switch the light on.
10. Touch your hair.
11. Take your coat off.
12. Stop the CD player.

1.21
eleven twelve thirteen fourteen fifteen sixteen seventeen eighteen nineteen twenty thirty forty fifty sixty seventy eighty ninety
a hundred   a hundred and one   a hundred and two
two hundred   three hundred   nine hundred
a thousand

1.22
1. ten
2. thirty
3. forty
4. fifteen
5. sixteen
6. seventy
7. eighty
8. nineteen
9. a hundred

1.23
Sam   What's your mobile number?
Andy It's 6974201720.
Sam   And your landline?
Andy 1603 664473.
Sam   What's your home address?
Andy 82, George Street, Norwich NR2 1LT, UK.
Sam   Are you on Facebook?
Andy Yeah, I've got 245 Facebook friends.
Sam   Wow! And what's your email?
Andy andy.maxwell@quickwebnet.uk
Sam   Thanks. What's your favourite colour, Andy?
Andy Red.
Sam   Okay, and your favourite number?
Andy 7.

1.24
twenty-second   forty-third   thirteenth

1.25
1. The first day of the week is Sunday.
2. The seventh day of the week is Saturday.
3. The third day of the week is Tuesday.
4. The sixth day of the week is Friday.
5. The fifth day of the week is Thursday.
6. The fourth day of the week is Wednesday.
7. The second day of the week is Monday.

1.26
1. It's five o'clock.
2. It's a quarter past eleven.
3. It's half past two.
4. It's a quarter to eight.

1.27
1. comb
2. notebook
3. ticket
4. map
5. digital camera
6. diary
7. laptop
8. keys
9. pen
10. wallet
11. MP3 player
12. mobile phone
13. cash card
14. pencils
15. passport

1.28
What is the LAC?
The London Arts Centre is a famous film school for young people in central London. We have got excellent courses for actors, directors, designers, writers and technicians and we've got state-of-the-art technology and professional, experienced teachers.
- digital cameras for students
- video cameras for students
- laptop computers for all students
- access to film, animation and recording studios
- film library with 5,000 films

Who are our students?
The LAC isn't only a British school, it's an international school with students from all over the world. We've got students from Europe, Asia, Africa and America and of course from Britain! The classes are small and informal and all students for us are special.

Who are the directors of the school?
Hannah Hill, our new Academy Director, is a famous American producer and scriptwriter with years of experience at the Kerner Brothers studios in Hollywood. Hannah is also the teacher on the film writing course this year.
Tony Harrison our Assistant Director has got 20 years of experience in the theatres of London's West End as an actor and director. Tony is the drama and voice teacher at the school.

Audioscripts

1.29

Antonio	Hi, I'm Antonio. What's your name?
Michael	Oh hello, I'm Michael. Where are you from? Are you Spanish?
Antonio	No, I'm from Liverpool, but my mum's Italian.
Michael	Italian? Where's she from?
Antonio	Rome. What about you?
Michael	I'm from Manchester.
Antonio	Manchester, wow! You've got a great football team!
Michael	Yeah, they're good. Have you got a place to stay, Antonio?
Antonio	Yeah, I've got a room with a family. What about you?
Michael	I've got an uncle and an aunt in London. And a cousin! Their house is huge – I've got a room there…
Antonio	Great! By the way, this is Robyn. She's Scottish. Robyn, this is Michael.
Michael	Hi, Robyn. Nice to meet you.
Robyn	And this is Anna Harrison. She's from London. Her parents have got a B&B here.
Antonio	B&B?
Robyn	Yeah, you know, a 'Bed and Breakfast', the Victoria Palace Hotel.
Michael	Anna, who's the man at the bar? Is he an actor?
Anna	No, he isn't. He's Tony Harrison, he's my uncle, my dad's brother. He's the assistant director of the LAC. He's cool!
Tony	Hello students, and welcome to the London Arts Centre…

1.30

This is Julia Jolly the American actress. Her father Jack and her husband Pete Brad are actors too. She's got one brother James, he's 35, and she has got a sister, Marion, and a stepsister, Elizabeth. Julia and Pete have got five children, a son called Zanox, a daughter called Zeeba, and twins called Nox and Venus. They've also got a baby girl called Shamana.

1.31

Hi, I'm Lucy. I've got a brother, Sam and a sister, Jenny. My mother's name is Sally and my father's name is Mark. My dad has got a brother – my uncle Steve. Steve's wife is my aunt Jane. They've got one daughter – my cousin Julia. My grandmother's name is Victoria and my grandfather is called Joseph.

1.32

house   his   holiday   her   here   have   husband   hotel

1.33

1 hit
2 at
3 hear
4 hand
5 air
6 eat
7 his

1.34

1 a hit
2 b at
3 b hear
4 b hand
5 b air
6 a eat
7 a his

1.35

Claudia	London's got restaurants from all over the world and Italian food especially is very popular here, particularly pizza!
Friend	Have they got food from Italy in the shops?
Claudia	Yes, in the supermarkets there's pasta, pizza, ragù, pesto… And there's food from other countries too: China, India, Thailand, Greece. It's really international.
Friend	What about coffee? The British are famous for terrible coffee!
Claudia	Not now! They've got hundreds of cafés now with cappuccino, espresso, latte… Italian coffee is very trendy!

1.36

Every month, we talk to people with interesting jobs. This month, we talk to Rosa Barrios from Barcelona.
In summertime we see lots of buskers in our cities. They play music and sing in the street for money, they dance, they paint. Rosa Barrios is 19 and she's Spanish but she lives in London, in a small bedsit in Camden. Rosa is a student and she does a very unusual job on Sundays.
'I work in the city centre. You see, I'm a living statue', she says, 'It's not easy but it's a very interesting job.'
Rosa gets up late at about 10 o'clock and she doesn't have breakfast. She has a shower then she gets dressed.
Does she wear special clothes for her job? 'Yes, I do. I've got a fantastic flamenco costume,' she says, 'With lots of different colours, or I wear my Tutankhamon costume.' Then she gets on her bike and she goes to work. 'I go to Leicester Square or Trafalgar Square, it depends. I find a good place and I don't move for hours, I usually stay there from midday to three. Children stop and smile, or tease me.'
Do people give her money when she works? 'Yes,' says Rosa, 'It's a good job. I make a lot of money.'
What do her family and friends think? 'Well, my mum and dad don't like my job but my friends think I'm very brave. And when people see me on my bike in my flamenco costume they think, 'Wow!'

1.37

I get up at ten to eight every morning and then I have a shower at about eight. I eat some cereal for breakfast, then I go to school with my mum in her car. My school starts at nine o'clock and we have lessons until lunchtime, that's at a quarter to one. I finish school at half past three and then I go home. After school I do my homework from about five o'clock to six, and in the evening after dinner I watch TV until about half past nine. Most nights I go to bed at a quarter to ten.

1.38

Anna	That's our B&B.
Antonio	It's nice. Do you live there?
Anna	Yes, I do. What about your house in London, is it nice?
Antonio	Yes, it's great. I've got a bedsit in the attic with a double bed in it. Robyn's got a room there too.
Anna	Cool! And does the landlady make your breakfast?
Robyn	No, she doesn't, we make our breakfast!
Anna	What about you, Mike? Have you got a big room in your aunt's house?
Michael	Not really. It's a typical London house and my room's a bit small, but it's cosy. There's a bed in it and a desk, a big TV, a wardrobe for my clothes… Oh, and there's a sofa bed for friends, too!

Audioscripts

Anna	Wicked! And do you like London, Mike?
Michael	I love London – there are hundreds of things to do! – but I don't go out in the evenings, I study! What about you, Anna?
Anna	I work, so I get up early and go to bed late!
Antonio	Wow! Have you got a job?
Anna	Yes, I have. I work for my dad in the B&B. I want to do the course at the LAC, but there are… problems. Dad doesn't like the idea.
Antonio	Bummer!

1.39

In the utility room:
1 washing machine

In the kitchen:
2 fridge
3 hob
4 cupboard
5 shelves
6 oven
7 sink

In the living room:
8 fireplace
9 bookcase
10 armchair
11 lamp

In the bedroom:
12 curtain
13 wardrobe
14 carpet
15 bedside table

In the bathroom:
16 washbasin
17 shower

1.40

1 chimney
2 garden
3 roof
4 window
5 door
6 gate
7 garage
8 hedge

1.41

/s/   talks
/iz/ washes
/z/   spends

1.42

watches looks studies takes prefers knows brushes
dresses makes buys

1.43

/s/   talks   looks   takes   makes
/iz/ washes   watches brushes dresses
/z/   studies prefers knows   buys

1.44

Intv	Tarbak, you're from Canada, is that right?
Tarbak	Yes, I live in the north of Canada in a small village in Nuova Scotia.
Intv	Do you live there all year?
Tarbak	No, in summer I go to live in a cabin near the sea with my family. We go fishing and hunting there. In winter we go back to the village – we have a modern house there and a car.
Intv	What's a typical day for you in the summer?
Tarbak	Well, I get up early in the morning – about 5 o'clock – and I get dressed then go out fishing.
Intv	You don't have breakfast?
Tarbak	No, I have breakfast later. I cook some of the fish I catch and I eat it for breakfast. Then we go home and give the rest of the fish to my mother. She prepares it to eat in the winter.
Intv	What do you do in the afternoons?
Tarbak	In the afternoons I go out in my boat with my father, brothers and uncles to look for whales. If we see one we hunt it, but they're difficult to catch. It's dangerous.
Intv	And in the evening? Do you have television?
Tarbak	No, not in the cabin but we watch TV in the winter in my village house. In the summer we meet friends and relatives from other villages. We eat together and we sing and talk and tell stories…

1.45

Most kids always go on holiday with their families. They go to a hotel or an apartment, they visit monuments on 'educational' trips and they sometimes go to eat in restaurants. Okay, maybe young kids enjoy all that but for a teenager, how often do you hear them say, 'It's soooo boring!'?!

I'm 16 now and I don't like going on holiday with my parents every year. I want to go with my friends sometimes; I like doing fun things – teenage things! My parents always say, 'No Robbie, come with us to Cornwall,' (they go to Cornwall every year!). But this year is different! I've got some money from my Saturday job and I've got a plan – a study camp holiday in the USA!

The camp is in Vermont and the programme looks fantastic! In the morning there are study courses in Art, Music and Drama (okay, I don't usually like lessons but I don't mind these courses – they're cool!). In the afternoon, there are outdoor activities – you play sports or go rafting, canoeing, wind-surfing… (I love water sports!), sometimes you feel lazy, so you just sunbathe and swim in the lake and stuff. They often organize camping trips too – you go by horse and sleep in tents in the forest! Wicked!

The accommodation is similar to a youth hostel – you sleep in a big room and everyone helps to cook the meals and clean up. The students come from all over the world – it's great! – I love meeting people from other countries and making new friends…

1.46

1 camper
2 tent
3 youth hostel
4 hotel
5 bed and breakfast
6 apartment

1.47

Michael	Hi, Robyn. You're late!
Robyn	Yeah, the Tube's really crowded now – I can't stand it! And the trains are often late.
Michael	Yeah, it's a real pain… I prefer the bus.
Antonio	Really? But the buses are usually late too! I always go by bike!
Robyn	Oh, no! You know me – I hate cycling in traffic! Where's Anna, Mike? I don't see her…
Michael	She's late too – it's this terrible rain! She wants to meet us in Leicester Square.
Robyn	Does she? How do you get to Leicester Square from here?
Michael	I think it's on the Piccadilly line. Let's ask…
Michael	Excuse me, do the trains on this line stop at Leicester Square?
Woman	No, they don't, dear. This is the Central line. For Leicester Square take the Central line for three stops, then change at Holborn station. Look.

119

Audioscripts

Michael	Holborn, okay...
Woman	At Holborn you take the Piccadilly line – it's the blue line.
Michael	Does the Piccadilly train go straight to Leicester Square?
Woman	Yes, it does. It's two stops.
Michael	That's great, thanks very much.
Woman	You're welcome.

1.48

1. train
2. bike
3. car
4. motorbike
5. bus
6. ship
7. taxi
8. van
9. ferry

1.49

1. A Does this train go to London?
   B Yes, it does.
   A Does it stop at York?
   B No, it doesn't.
2. A Excuse me, do all these buses go to the city centre?
   B No, they don't. You want the 32 or the 11.
   A Okay, thanks.
3. A How do you get to the railway station from here?
   B Take the number 25 bus for four stops. It's opposite the Grand Hotel.

1.50

/ŋ/ thing wing bang swimming playing
/n/ thin win ban swim in play in

1.51

ring relax in stink lying Ron van relaxing rang wrong lie in

1.52

/ŋ/ ring stink lying relaxing rang wrong
/n/ relax in Ron van lie in

1.53

Jill	What's your book, Martin?
Martin	It's *The Great Railway Bazaar* by Paul Theroux.
Jill	Is it good?
Martin	Yeah, I really like it. He's a good writer.
Jill	What's it about?
Martin	It's about travelling across India by train.
Jill	It's a travel book then?
Martin	Yeah, but it's also funny.
Jill	Do you often read travel books?
Martin	Yes, I do. I think they're interesting You learn a lot about other countries and cultures and stuff. What about you, Jill?
Gill	I prefer detective stories – I love Agatha Christie's books!
Martin	Really? What's your favourite book then?
Jill	Er... I think *Murder on the Orient Express*. Do you know it?
Martin	Yeah, well... I remember the film...
Jill	Do you? Well the story is set in the 1920s and it's about a train journey too.
Martin	Who are the main characters?
Jill	Well, there's Hercule Poirot of course and then there's...

1.54

Trend	In this week's *Trend* interview, we ask teenagers on the streets of Britain, 'What are you wearing today – and why?' Jessica, you're wearing very trendy clothes – jeans, a red hoodie, a vest top and trainers. What a cool look! Why do you like these clothes?
Jessica	Well, I'm wearing jeans because they're comfortable and I'm wearing this top because it's skater-style.
Trend	Johnny, you're wearing skateboarding clothes too, right?
Johnny	Yeah, that's right. Jessica and I are into skater stuff.
Trend	Are you wearing those shorts because it's hot, or because they're trendy?!
Johnny	Because I really like the colour!
Trend	I see. Cool. Billy, you aren't wearing trendy clothes today! Is that your school uniform?
Billy	Yes, our uniform at Green Park School is this blue jumper, white shirt, grey trousers and tie.
Trend	Do you like wearing school uniform?
Billy	It's not very cool, but it's only for school. I don't mind it. In the evening I always wear a tracksuit and trainers! I'm not very interested in clothes.
Trend	And you, Beatrice?
Beatrice	Well, I hate the skirt and white socks – I look like a kid! – but the uniform is practical. I love clothes – especially shoes! – but I keep my designer stuff for weekends. I'm shopping for a new dress and sandals now – for an eighteenth birthday party.
Trend	Enjoy your shopping then!
Beatrice	Thanks!

1.55

1. shirt
2. jacket
3. trousers
4. shoes
5. skirt
6. dress
7. coat
8. jumper
9. trainers

1.56

1. Laura is wearing leggings, a T-shirt, trainers, and black sunglasses.
2. Valerie is wearing a dress with a belt, a green scarf and cowboy boots.
3. Richard is wearing a coat, a shirt with a red and blue tie, brown gloves and a black hat.

1.57

Assistant	Can I help you?
Anna	Yes, please. Can I try this top on?
Assistant	Sure. Anything else?
Anna	I'm looking for a miniskirt too.
Assistant	Yes certainly, what size are you looking for?
Anna	Size 10.
Assistant	What about this style? It's casual and we've got it in floral cotton too.
Anna	Oh, yes, what a lovely style! Have you got it in other colours?
Anna	Hi, Dad. I'm going out now.
Dad	Are you going out again?
Anna	Yes Dad, I always go out on Friday. It's my night off.
Dad	Are you wearing that skirt?
Anna	Yes, I am. It's new – I've got a date...
Dad	A date?

Audioscripts

Anna	Bye. See you at twelve.
Dad	At twelve midnight?
Anna	Dad, I'm 16! Anyway, Antonio's waiting for me. Bye!

1.58

1	smart	7	striped
2	tight	8	loose
3	floral	9	patterned
4	plain	10	cotton
5	checked	11	woollen
6	casual	12	leather

1.59

/tʃ/	cheap choose chilling much catch
/ʃ/	shirt shoes shilling hush cash

1.60

sheep church check shower sure touch show furniture children push

1.61

/tʃ/	church check touch furniture children
/ʃ/	sheep shower sure show push

1.62

I work in one of the shops at the British Museum in London. It's a beautiful place inside the central court of the museum, and the work is interesting because every day you meet people from all over the world. We sell souvenirs of the Museum collections – bags, pens, notebooks, that sort of thing – but we also do beautiful copies of ancient jewellery, coins, vases and statues in the collection. We've got a lot of books in the shop – particularly about History, Archaeology and Art – and we sell toys and puzzles for children too.

2.02

1 The favourite dish in the UK is now chicken tikka masala, a curry dish of roast chicken in a red, spicy, tomato sauce.
2 It isn't true that there isn't much variety in the British diet, the British love eating foreign food and especially popular are Italian, Chinese and Thai food. There are also a lot of ready-made foreign dishes in supermarkets and restaurants and the new fast food in Britain today is sushi!
3 There are some very expensive restaurants but fish and chips costs just a few pounds! There are also Indian and Chinese restaurants – they serve cheap, tasty food.
4 Traditional British dishes are also popular – many chefs only use local British ingredients to make them in their restaurants. Most pubs and hotels also serve traditional dishes like roast beef and Yorkshire pudding, Lancashire hotpot and apple crumble.
5 At home, most people usually have a light breakfast – coffee or tea and toast or cereal – but some people eat more at weekends. Hotels and cafés serve the traditional 'Full English Breakfast' of bacon, sausage, eggs, tomatoes and mushrooms but it's for the tourists!
6 Tea is originally from India but of course it's the favourite drink in Britain. The British love tea – with milk and a little sugar! Some people drink 6 or 7 cups a day!

2.03

sausages bacon eggs beans milk cheese toast
cereal mushrooms tea coffee yoghurt pasta
fruit juice pastries cake tomatoes biscuits

2.04

Anna	Yuk! There's too much sugar in this coffee!
Antonio	And there isn't any sugar in my coffee! Yuk!
Anna	I think this is your coffee, Antonio! Swap?
Antonio	Okay. Mmm… that's better. Now, the shopping. Have we got any cereal?
Anna	Well, there isn't much…
Antonio	Okay. Three packets of cereal. Now, are there any eggs?
Anna	Well, there are few… but there aren't enough for breakfast.
Antonio	How many eggs are there?
Anna	Not many – four.
Antonio	Let's get three dozen.
Anna	No, three dozen are too many, Antonio! Two dozen are enough.
Antonio	Okay, you're the boss. Are there any sausages?
Anna	Yes, there are enough sausages, I think, but there isn't much cheese.
Antonio	Right, a kilo of cheese…
Anna	No, that's too much cheese! Write half a kilo.
Antonio	Half a kilo of cheese. And how much sugar is there?
Anna	Sugar? There's a lot of sugar – look! Four packets!
Antonio	'Ah, sugar, sugar, you are my candy girl…'
Anna	Antonio, stop it! Dad's coming.
Henry	What's going on here?
Anna	Nothing. Antonio's helping me, Dad.

2.05

1	a jar of jam	6	a can of cola
2	a bottle of water	7	a tin of beans
3	a loaf of bread	8	a packet of biscuits
4	a bag of apples	9	a slice of cake
5	a carton of fruit juice		

2.06

Mrs Granger	Good morning, is that Fresco's supermarket?
Manager	Yes, madam, it is. How can I help you?
Mrs Granger	It's my online shopping order. This week a lot of things are missing…
Manager	I'm very sorry, madam. Which items are missing?
Mrs Granger	Well, there's too much cereal – four packets but I only need two – and there isn't any cheese. And there isn't much milk – just one carton but I need three. Then there aren't any biscuits or yoghurt but there's a lot of bacon.
Manager	How much bacon is there?
Mrs Granger	Three packets.
Manager	And how many packets of biscuits do you want?
Mrs Granger	Two packets.
Manager	Right. Anything else?
Mrs Granger	Yes, I need a tin of coffee – 450 grams – and a loaf of bread but I don't want the eggs. There are a dozen eggs! Then there's too much…

2.07

problem water receive record

121

Audioscripts

2.08
bacon   coffee   biscuit   believe   complete   shopping   enjoy   packet   compare   create   prefer   carton   apple   bottle

2.09
First column: bacon, coffee, biscuit, shopping, packet, carton, apple, bottle.
Second column: believe, complete, enjoy, compare, create, prefer

2.10
In English cuisine there's a lot of variety. Many British people like foreign food. There are some fast food restaurants in the UK but there also a lot of Italian, Indian and Chinese restaurants. Nowadays at home British people don't eat much for breakfast. They usually have coffee or tea and toast or cereal. But in many hotels they still serve the 'Full English Breakfast' – and that is a lot of food!! Tea is still the favourite drink in England. The British love tea and they drink a lot of cups of tea – about 6 every day!

2.11
Simon Doctor Hall, good afternoon. Tell me, what are your main worries about GM food?
Dr Hall Well, Simon, scientists now know that GM crops often contaminate other crops.
Simon Contaminate other crops? How?
Dr Hall Genetically modified super-plants like soya beans, potatoes, corn and sugar start to dominate the ecosystem because they are strong and resistant to diseases. They grow fast and they grow everywhere! Other plants die because of this and that means there is no diversity or variety in the plant life in a particular area.
Simon I see.
Dr Hall This also means that insects and animals die because they can't find the plants they like to eat.
Simon What about any negative effects on humans?
Dr Hall Well, GM crops sometimes cause allergies. Many doctors believe that more people now suffer from allergies to pollen because of GM crops.
Simon Because they produce new types of pollen?
Dr Hall Yes, exactly. Humans are sensitive to these new types of super-strong pollen. But the main worry for most of us about GM technology is the future. Do we really understand all the possible effects on humans of these new super-plants? The technology is evolving very fast and scientists don't have time to test all the effects before these foods arrive in shops and supermarkets. We want to know: Is GM food really safe?

2.12
Millions of kids all over the world enjoy watching TV talent shows. But now you too can be in a show! Most young people can only dream of fame and fortune but now that fantasy is becoming a reality for hundreds of British teenagers.

You too can make it!!
Do you think you've got talent?
Can you show your skills on national television?
Can you impress the judges and our studio audience?
Do you enjoy media attention?
Are you looking for the chance to start a career in showbiz?

Your big opportunity!
Why don't you audition for *Teens Have Got Talent*? What are you waiting for?
This show is for you, teenagers aged 13-19! Are you thinking, 'But I can't sing, I haven't got any talent'? Not true!! What about your other abilities? Can you dance? Can you tell jokes? Do magic? Write screenplays for television? Are you a composer or an actor? This is your chance to show us what you can do! The acts we choose from the local auditions go on to perform on one of our weekly TV programmes. The judges and our TV audience then choose the best acts to go on to the final, and the winner performs in front of Her Majesty the Queen in our final Christmas Extravaganza!

Why don't you come to an audition and try?
To participate in the auditions please send us:
- a recent photo
- a few words about you
- a brief description of your act
- a two-minute film clip of your act
- your email address and mobile number

2.13
1 d actor/actress   acts in films
2 a director   directs films
3 g photographer   takes photographs
4 b cameraman   uses a video or film camera
5 c painter   paints pictures
6 f composer   writes music
7 h singer   sings songs for an audience

2.14
Hannah Now, Anna, tell me about yourself.
Anna Sure. Err…
Hannah Let's start with films. Why do you want to come to the LAC?
Anna I love the cinema. It's magic. But I don't just want to watch films, I want to be in them!
Hannah Really? You want to be an actress then? And what about the Performing Arts? Can you dance?
Anna Yes, I can dance quite well. I go to modern dance classes on Wednesdays and Saturdays.
Hannah Good. You're a ballerina too! Can you play any musical instruments?
Anna No, I can't play music at all but I can sing really well. My singing teacher says I've got a great voice. At weekends I sing in a bar in Covent Garden with three friends. We've got a blues band.
Hannah What about languages? Can you speak any foreign languages?
Anna Yes, I can. I can speak French. And I'm learning Italian.
Hannah Really? Other interests or hobbies?
Anna I like making clothes and I enjoy taking photographs. I'm doing a photography course at the Arts Centre at the moment.
Hannah Excellent! Can you use a video camera?
Anna No, I can't, but I'm sure I can learn…
Hannah Right. Is there anything else you can do?
Anna Well… there's cooking. I'm good at cooking. I help in the kitchen of my parents' B&B.
Hannah Okay, cooking is creative. Let's write that too.

Audioscripts

2.15
1 do motocross
2 make models
3 listen to music
4 play chess
5 play snooker
6 collect cards
7 chat online
8 make clothes
9 go rollerblading

2.16
Mr Girotti So, James, what can you do?
James I'm good at basketball and I can play the guitar…
Mr Girotti Yes but, err… for example, can you drive a car? It's important for this job.
James I can't drive a car but I can drive a scooter. I've got a Vespa.
Mr Girotti Excellent! Now, do you know the town centre well? Can you find the streets easily?
James Oh yes, I live in King Street – it's right in the centre. I know every street in town!
Mr Girotti Fantastic! Are you good at Maths? You need to take the money and give change to customers when you deliver their pizzas.
James No problem, I'm really good at maths. It's my favourite subject!
Mr Girotti Great! Can you start tomorrow?
James Yes, I can! Of course. Thanks!

2.17
1 Which sports can you play?
2 I can play the piano.
3 He can't swim.

2.18
/æ/ can pan Ann hat
/aː/ can't plant aunt heart

2.19
apple start bag man tomato car banana bat

2.20
/æ/ apple bag man bat
/aː/ start tomato car banana

2.21
Intv Hello and welcome to Radio Alison! Today we've got some special guests in the studio, Teresa and Tommy. Hi guys! Can you tell us what it is that you do?
Teresa Hi! Well, we're both studying acting at drama college in Leeds but in our free time we're also members of a brand new band, The Birds.
Intv So, what type of music do The Birds play?
Teresa Well, we usually play ska and reggae. Both types of music come from Jamaica, where my family comes from, but we prefer ska really.
Tom Yeah! With ska you can play fast and really loud! It's mental!
Intv Ska music? Cool! How many musicians are there in the band?
Teresa Well, at the moment there are four of us. I'm the singer and Tom plays the guitar.
Tom I can play the saxophone quite well too, but I can't sing. I'm really bad at singing!
Intv Which other musicians are there in the band?
Teresa Well, there's Jake, our bass guitar player. He composes our songs too – he's really good at writing songs and our fans' favourite songs are all Jake's – and he plays the piano. Then there's Phil – he plays the drums.
Intv Where can people hear your music? Have you got a CD?
Teresa No, we haven't got any albums out yet but you can visit our website or come to one of our gigs!
Intv Can I ask you why you decided to form a band?
Tom Well, it was really because…

2.22
1 be born
2 go to school
3 find a job
4 get married
5 have children
6 retire

2.23
1 The annual festival for lovers is…
   a Valentine's Day.
2 Which actors were the two lovers in the film *Titanic*?
   a Leonardo DiCaprio and Kate Winslet.
3 In which of these films were there two lovers, Bella Swan and Edward Cullen, with very long teeth?
   c *Twilight*.
4 In the play *Romeo and Juliet* by William Shakespeare what happens to the two lovers?
   c They die.
5 Which of these hit songs wasn't a love song?
   b *Holiday*, Green Day.
6 The symbol of love in Celtic civilisation was…
   b a knot.
7 Which of these beautiful women was the cause of the Trojan War?
   b Helen.
8 Can you complete these famous comments about love?
   'All you need is love.' *song by John Lennon & Paul McCartney.*
   'Love means not ever having to say you're sorry.' *Erich Segal in the novel 'Love Story'.*

2.24
eyes: brown, grey, black, blue, green
hair: fair, dark, red, grey, black, brown, curly, straight, short, long
height: short, tall
other: big, small, plump, plain, pretty, slim

2.25
1 c plump – slim
2 d tall – short
3 e pretty – plain
4 b small – big
5 a fair – dark
6 g straight – curly
7 f short – long

2.26
Henry Where were you last night? You were late. It was after midnight…
Anna Well, it's a bit complicated. I was with my friends and…
Henry What about this morning? You were asleep until 10 o'clock. You can't stay in bed all morning! We need you in the kitchen. There were a lot of people at breakfast.
Anna Look, Dad, I'm 16 now…
Henry Yes, but you can't stay out till midnight! Were you in a bar? You're an intelligent girl, you know you can't go to bars at 16.
Anna I wasn't in a bar! I was at a pizza restaurant. Dad, give me a break!
Hilary What's going on you two?

123

Audioscripts

Henry Anna was out last night and she wasn't here to help with the breakfast this morning! She's irresponsible!
Hilary Well, Henry, it was Anna's night off…
Anna And I'm not a little girl any more!
Hilary Now, now, Anna… You weren't here to clean the bedrooms yesterday either.
Anna I'm sorry Mum. I had an interview.
Henry An interview? For a job?!
Anna No, for the London Arts Centre. I want to be an actress!

2.27

irresponsible silly intelligent friendly shy talkative quiet reliable sensible responsible polite calm funny nervous rude

2.28

Who was Marilyn Monroe?
Marilyn's real name was Norma Jeane Baker and she was born on June 1, 1926. Her first job was in a factory; then she was a model. Her first acting roles were small, for example she had a very small role in the Marx Brothers film *Love Happy* in 1949. She was a talented actress and won some important awards. She was the winner of the David di Donatello prize, the Italian Oscar (in 1956), and a Golden Globe for her role in the comedy *Some Like it Hot*.
Marilyn was a good comic actress but she was also intelligent – she studied Art and Literature at the University of California. Her friends say she was shy, very sweet and clever.
Marilyn was a very beautiful woman and was famous for her blue eyes and blonde hair in her films, but her real hair was brown. She married three times, first to James Dougherty, a police officer, then to Joe DiMaggio (real name Giuseppe Paolo DiMaggio) a great American baseball player. Her third husband was Arthur Miller, the famous playwright.
In her final years she was very ill. She was anxious and afraid and her death at 36 years old is still a mystery. Was it suicide, was it an accident or was it murder? We don't know the truth.

2.29

1 hair
2 eyebrow
3 forehead
4 ear
5 eye
6 cheek
7 nose
8 mouth
9 teeth
10 chin

2.30

responsible, polite, important
irresponsible, impolite, unimportant

2.31

1 relevant
2 reliable
3 practical
4 responsive
5 intelligent
6 mature
7 rational
8 attractive
9 perfect

2.32

1 irrelevant
2 unreliable
3 impractical
4 unresponsive
5 unintelligent
6 immature
7 irrational
8 unattractive
9 imperfect

2.33

David Mr Turner, who was Pocahontas?
Mr Turner Pocahontas? Well David, she was a Native American princess. She's famous because she was the first Native American to go and live in Britain and she was an ambassador for Native American culture.
David When was she born?
Mr Turner She was born around 1595, I think.
David Really? 400 years ago! Was she from the Wild West?
Mr Turner No, her father was an important chief of many tribes in the area which is now Virginia, on the east coast of the United States. The British were at war with the Native American tribes then.
David Was she a soldier?
Mr Turner No, she wasn't but when she was a teenager the British soldiers took her prisoner. In prison, she learned to speak English and started to talk to the British about her people and their culture, and to promote peace between the two countries.
David Was she married?
Mr Turner Yes, she was. She fell in love with an Englishman, John Rolfe, in Virginia, and married him. They had a son, too. She died in 1617 when he was still a baby.
David So she was really the first Native American woman to work for better relations between white Europeans and ethnic minorities?
Mr Turner That's right, David, she was!

2.34

1 This is a photo of our boat trip on the River Thames last Tuesday – it rained a bit but we enjoyed it – it was really relaxing and we saw a lot of famous places including the London Eye. At the end, we visited the Houses of Parliament. (That was a bit boring!) We wanted to visit Big Ben but it was closed to visitors.
2 …We watched the ceremony of the Changing of the Guard outside Buckingham Palace last weekend. It took place at 11.30 and Antonio missed it because he arrived late! Then we went to the Tate Modern; it was an old power station but now it's an art gallery. It's really cool! The things there are weird but fascinating – I studied some of them in Art at school last term. We finished Sunday afternoon with some shopping in Oxford Street (zzzz!!) and Robyn bought some souvenirs.
3 Antonio wanted to go on a walking tour yesterday so we did the 'Mystery Walk'. We followed the trail of Jack the Ripper and we visited some places where famous crimes happened (but they weren't very frightening!). That part lasted two hours and was quite tiring. They also showed us the house of someone famous in Baker Street: the house is a museum now… Who lived there? I can't remember! Anyway, it was really interesting but we walked and walked. We were sooooo tired!

2.35

It was… boring, tiring, fascinating, frightening, interesting, exciting, relaxing.
I was… bored, tired, fascinated, frightened, interested, excited, relaxed.

2.36

Anna Hi! Did you enjoy your sightseeing this morning?
Robyn Oh, yes. I loved it. It was really interesting!
Anna Who did you go with?

Audioscripts

Robyn I was with Antonio and Michael. Why didn't you come?
Anna Oh, I had stuff to do… Anyway, what did you see in London?
Robyn Well, we went to Buckingham Palace to see the Changing of the Guard.
Anna Oh no! Boring!!
Robyn No, it was cool. I took some great photos.
Anna Did you go to the Tate Modern?
Robyn Yes, we did. A bit boring.
Anna Oh, I think it's fascinating!
Robyn Anyway, the café was really amazing – great design. Then we did some shopping…
Anna What did you buy?
Robyn Well, Antonio bought some jeans and a T-shirt but Michael didn't buy anything.
Anna What about you?
Robyn I bought Big Ben, Buckingham Palace and a double-decker bus.
Anna Very funny, Robyn.
Robyn No really, look. I got them for my nephew. He's only eight! What about you? You look a bit upset!
Anna Actually I didn't have a good day. I feel depressed. I had another row with my dad.
Robyn What happened?
Anna Oh, he doesn't want me to go out, to see my friends, to go to the LAC…
Robyn You're kidding! Why not?
Anna It's a long story…

2.37

embarrassed jealous angry surprised worried annoyed happy scared bored upset depressed nervous

2.38

We walked a lot. We visited Blackfriars – William Shakespeare bought a house there or something. That was a bit boring. I preferred Baker Street – They say Sherlock Holmes lived at number 221B. It is a museum now. But Sherlock Holmes didn't really live there; it's just a story.
We also saw Oscar Wilde's house in Chelsea. He lived there with his wife and two children.
We visited Charles Dickens' house – the guide said he wrote *Oliver Twist* there… I was really tired by then.
My favourite visit was Westminster Tube Station – they made some scenes from *Harry Potter* there, it was brilliant!

2.39

emotions: bored, interested, excited, tired, relaxed, amused, annoyed, worried, fascinated
things/events/people: boring, interesting, exciting, tiring, relaxing, amusing, annoying, worrying, fascinating

2.40

/t/	looked	watched
/ɪd/	visited	ended
/d/	played	lived

2.41

/t/	walked	looked
/ɪd/	started	recorded
/d/	danced	showed

2.42

1 A I like Paris, but it's expensive.
   B And the French are a bit unfriendly.
2 A Let's go for a pizza, I'm hungry.
   B Now? It's a bit late.
3 A She wasn't very good at the interview.
   B No, but she was a bit nervous and the questions were difficult.

2.43

Toby Dr Henshaw, you are an expert on 19th century occupations and some of them were quite unusual, weren't they?
Dr Henshaw Yes, Toby, they were. Many of them don't exist today, mudlarks, for example.
Toby Mudlarks?
Dr Henshaw Yes, they were er… children…err… they worked on the mud of the River Thames looking for things in the river.
Toby Really? What sort of things?
Dr Henshaw Coins and jewellery or sometimes clothes. They also collected wood, you know, for fires.
Toby Was it a dangerous job?
Dr Henshaw Sometimes, yes. Children often fell into the water and died. That made the rivermen happy!
Toby Why? What did the rivermen do?
Dr Henshaw Well Toby, in those days, there were often dead bodies in the river. London was a dangerous and violent place and it was common for thieves to murder their victims and throw them into the river. Rivermen operated from the banks in boats. They pulled the corpses from the water with long hooks, took any valuable things from their pockets, then threw them back into the water.
Toby That's terrible!
Dr Henshaw Yes but then there were also the toshers. Toshers went down into the sewers and looked for valuable things there.
Toby They worked in the sewers! Ugh!
Dr Henshaw Yes, not surprisingly the toshers were not popular with the neighbours! Many of them became rich, but they always smelled of the sewers. Terrible!

2.44

Did you know that many of the great discoveries or inventions in history happened by accident or 'serendipity' – when you discover something while you are actually trying to do something else? They say that Isaac Newton, the father of modern physics, finally understood gravity, after years of research, when an apple fell on his head one day as he was sitting reading under a tree in his garden! And Christopher Columbus wasn't actually looking for it when he discovered America – he arrived there while he was searching for India!

One day, in 1823, the pupils at a famous school in Rugby, England, were playing in a football match. The game was in full swing and of course everyone was running and kicking the ball. Then one of the players broke the rules. William Webb Ellis was running when someone passed the ball to him, but Ellis didn't kick the ball, he jumped up and caught it in his hands! His opponents were chasing him but he ran like the wind with the ball in his hands until he got to the goal. The spectators were cheering wildly and everyone agreed that Ellis's controversial technique was incredibly exciting. The teams decided to make a new set of rules for a new ball game and rugby football was born. Was this genius or serendipity?!

Audioscripts

2.45
1	scientist	7	sailor
2	doctor	8	engineer
3	lawyer	9	plumber
4	nurse	10	postman
5	architect	11	electrician
6	secretary	12	shop assistant

2.46

Robyn Anna's late.
Antonio I phoned her an hour ago.
Robyn What was she doing?
Antonio She was just leaving the house.
Robyn Here she is!
Anna Sorry I'm late, everyone.
Robyn What happened?
Anna It was awful! This guy mugged me.
Michael What? Someone mugged you?!
Robyn Oh my God! Poor you!
Anna Yes, in Regent Street. I was coming out of the Tube station when I noticed this guy behind me. He was looking at me a bit strangely, you know. Then as I was turning into Regent Street, he came up behind me and said something quietly. I turned around and suddenly he grabbed my bag. While we were struggling I shouted for help and after that he ran away towards Piccadilly Circus.
Robyn Did you get a good look at him? Could you describe him to the police?
Anna I couldn't see his face very well, it was getting dark.
Antonio What was he wearing?
Anna He was wearing a black hoodie and jeans.
Michael Was he young?
Anna About 20 I think. He took my bag and my mobile, so I couldn't even phone for help.
Antonio Were you carrying much money?
Anna No, I wasn't. Just a few pounds. But I feel really shaken.
Robyn Of course you do! Come on, let's go in and sit down.

2.47
1 mugger 2 robber 3 forger 4 thief

2.48
1	doctor	5	secretary
2	photograph	6	cupboard
3	sailor	7	robber
4	America	8	water

2.49
1 Look at the clock, it's a quarter to seven!
2 Remember to telephone your sister tomorrow.
3 Shall I send you another letter?
4 I was thinking about my wonderful trip to South America.

2.50

Teacher So what book did you read for the exam, Miranda?
Miranda I read *Frankenstein's Monster* by Mary Shelley.
Teacher Splendid! It's a great book, a classic. Can you tell me who the main characters are?
Miranda Yes, Dr Frankenstein is the main character and then there's the monster he creates in his laboratory.
Teacher And what is the story about? What are the main themes of the book?
Miranda It's about good and evil and what those words really mean. At first Frankenstein seems like the good guy and the monster seems like the bad guy, but later we understand that Frankenstein is the criminal because he created the monster without thinking about the consequences.
Teacher What can you tell me about the personality of Frankenstein? What type of man is he?
Miranda He's very ambitious – he wants to be famous and create something incredible. He's also selfish because he doesn't think about the effect his actions have on other people.
Teacher And what about the monster?
Miranda I think the monster is the victim in the story. He is basically good but he becomes bad because everyone he meets treats him badly because of how he looks. They only judge him on his appearance.
Teacher I see. Now what happens at the end of the story? …

2.51

What is e-shopping?
In these days of the Credit Crunch everything in the shops seems to be getting more expensive. Everyone is trying to save money. For the clever shopper the answer is simple: e-shopping. You can buy almost anything on the web now and it's quick, easy and convenient – you can do everything without even leaving your home! No more, 'But I can't find anywhere to park!' or, 'I can't stand waiting in this queue!' You can order from your sofa!

How does it work?
1 First find a website with the goods you're looking for. You can use a search engine like Google to do this.
2 Browse the lists of products and prices then choose something you want.
3 You may need to register on the site to order, some websites ask you to do this, some don't.
4 Complete the order form with the requested information about the type and quantity of goods you want, your delivery details and your credit card information. (Everyone needs a valid credit card or electronic payment card to pay for goods online.)
5 The company then sends you an email to confirm your order. Print it and put it somewhere safe – this is your receipt!

2.52
1 cash card 2 credit card 3 voucher 4 cheque
5 cash

2.53

Waiter Whose is the chicken?
Anna It isn't mine – I'm having fish.
Waiter Chicken with olives?
Michael Err, no. It isn't mine. I'm having the vegetarian lasagne.
Waiter Chicken for you, sir?
Antonio No, steak. I don't think the chicken is ours. Maybe it's for someone at another table?
Waiter Oh, I'm very sorry.
Michael No problem.

Waiter Whose is the fish? Anyone?
Antonio It's hers, Anna's.
Waiter And the vegetarian dish?
Anna That's his. Michael!

Audioscripts

Michael	Oh, thanks. It looks delicious!
Waiter	Is everyone having beer?
Anna	Err... no one wants beer, actually. Perhaps it's for the other table too?
Waiter	Oh, right. My apologies. Well, would you like anything to drink?
Anna	I'd like cola, please.
Antonio	And we'll have mineral water. Sparkling.
Anna	I haven't got any cutlery! Whose is this fork? Is it yours, Antonio?
Antonio	No, it's not mine. I haven't got any cutlery either!
Michael	Yeah, the food's good but the service is awful here!
Waiter	I'm sorry about the confusion, it's my first night.
Anna	Really? Don't worry about it, we're fine now.

2.54

Waiter	Are you ready to order?
Girl	Yes, we are. Can I have the steak please?
Waiter	Certainly. Would you like a side dish?
Girl	Yes, the roast potatoes, please.
Waiter	Fine. And you sir?
Boy	What's the fish of the day?
Waiter	It's tuna.
Boy	Mmm, good, I love tuna! Okay, I'll have the tuna, please.
Waiter	Any vegetables with the fish, sir?
Boy	Err, a green salad please.
Waiter	And would you like anything to drink?
Girl	Yes, some mineral water please.
Boy	And I'll have a cola.
Waiter	Right, thank you.

2.55

1. cup
2. knife
3. glass
4. bowl
5. fork
6. plate
7. spoon
8. napkin
9. salt and pepper
10. saucer

2.56

I want to take you to the library later.
Can I have a glass of water?

2.57

1. Is the butcher's next to the fish and chip shop?
2. She got out of bed and started to pack her bags.
3. Let's go to the seaside on Saturday!
4. Where did you put that pair of brown shoes?

2.58

Pres	Research shows that the average British teenager spends £12.40 a week on clothes, games, entertainment and personal items. Where do they get their money from? Our reporter Greg Winters interviewed some teens at Fairview Shopping Centre to find out what they do to earn money and what things they like to spend it on...
Greg	So Sophie, how much pocket money do you get every week?
Sophie	My dad gives me ten pounds a week.
Greg	And what do you usually spend it on?
Sophie	I buy accessories like earrings and bags but not clothes – my mum buys those for me. I buy music CDs and magazines too, and sometimes I use the money to go to the cimena or a fast food restaurant with my friends.
Greg	Hannah, what about you?
Hannah	I've got a Saturday job. I work in a baker's shop and I get fifteen pounds a week for that.
Greg	What do you spend the money on?
Hannah	I don't spend much of it, just a little on going out with my friends and presents for my family's birthdays and stuff. I'm trying to save the money so I can buy a motorbike soon. I live in the country but my school and all my friends are in town. I want to get some wheels!
Greg	Rajit, do you get pocket money?
Rajit	Yes, I do. My mother gives me six pounds a week plus I've got a job two evenings a week as a pizza delivery boy. I earn about twelve pounds a week doing that.
Greg	Do you save the money?
Rajit	I try to save about half of it, yes. The rest I spend on computer games, magazines and DVDs. Oh, and tickets for the football! I'm a big Chelsea fan!
Greg	Cool! Are you saving for anything in particular?
Rajit	I want to go to university when I finish school but it's expensive. My parents want to help but I need to have money for books and things too so ... every little helps!

Flash on English Elementary

Editorial project: Simona Franzoni
Editorial department: Pauline Carr, Sabina Cedraro, Linda Pergolini
Art Director: Marco Mercatali
Page design and layout: Sergio Elisei, Sara Blasigh
Picture Editor: Giorgia D'Angelo
Production Manager: Francesco Capitano

Cover

Cover design: Paola Lorenzetti
Photo: Shutterstock, Giuseppe Aquili *(left)*

© 2013 ELI S.r.l
P.O. Box 6
62019 Recanati
Italy
Tel. +39 071 750701
Fax. +39 071 977851
info@elionline.com
www.elionline.com

The Publisher would like to give a special thanks to Martha Huber for her precious contribution to this project.

No unauthorised photocopying

All rights reserved. No part of this publication may be reproduced, stored in a retrieval system, or transmitted, in any form or by any means, electronic, mechanical, photocopying, recording or otherwise, without the prior written permission of ELI.

This book is sold subject to the condition that it shall not, by way of trade or otherwise, be lent, resold, hired out, or otherwise circulated without the publisher's prior consent in any form of binding or cover than that in which it is published and without a similar condition being imposed on the subsequent purchaser.

While every effort has been made to trace all the copyright holders, if any have been inadvertently overlooked the publisher will be pleased to make the necessary arrangements at the first opportunity.

Printed by Tecnostampa – Recanati 13.83154.0

ISBN 978-88-536-1542-8

Acknowledgements

Illustrated by Laura Bresciani, Rodolfo Brocchini, Giovanni da Re, Simone Massoni e Ilaria Falorsi

Commissioned Photography and Production in London by Giuseppe Aquili: pp. 8, 26, 34, 36, 44, 52, 62, 70, 80, 88, 98
Photography and Production assistant: Anthony Dawton
London model agency: Allsorts Agency
The Publisher would like to thank Mill Hill School Enterprises, London; The Tower Tavern, London; Wimpy, Loughton; Frank's Coffee shop, London; Mortimer's Café, London; Market Place, London; Max C, London.

Photo acknowledgement
Archivio ELI: pp. 10, 11, 15, 30 (B-E), 35, 57 (B, top right), 69 (4-5-6), 74 (top right, bottom), 75 (bottom), 81 (top left), 86 (C).
Corbis: pp. 86 (B).
Fotolia: p. 50 (bottom)
Gettyimages: pp. 38 (top right B), 69 (top right 3-7), 102.
Kathleen Tyler Conkliin: p. 57 (D).
Marka: pp. 38 (top right A), 39 (D-E).
Olycom: pp. 10, 11, 15, 16, 78, 81 (top right).
Photos: pp. 20, 50 (bottom), 84, 85, 92 (A-C), 93.
Shutterstock: pp. 10, 11, 13, 15, 16, 17, 18, 19, 21, 23, 25, 29, 30 (A-C-D-F-G-H, bottom), 31, 32, 38 (top left A-B-C-D-E), 39 (C), 42, 43, 45, 50 (top), 53, 56, 57 (top right, middle), 60, 61, 63, 66, 67, 68, 69 (1-2-8), 71, 72, 74 (A-B-C-D-E-F), 79, 82, 86 (A-D), 87, 89, 96, 97, 104, 105, 107, 110, 111.